# DIVINE WONDER

## ABIDING IN THE UNSEEN

JONATHAN NELSON

# ACKNOWLEDGEMENTS

I had the privilege of being introduced to Laurie Nelson at Agapé Studios by Pastor Sonny Misar, a key leader in my life who worked with Laurie to release his book ***"Journey to Authenticity,"*** as well as other projects. Laurie is incredibly gifted, and she was so much fun to work with; this book would have never been complete without her. Thank you Laurie.

I'm beyond grateful for Pastor Bryan Ost and his wife, Helene, as well as Daniel Ojeda, Brandon Athey, Nichole Sny, Matthew Brizendine, Allison Wells, Renz Tormen, and Cowen Kuowen for generously contributing to get this message published.

Thank you, Pastor Toby Cavanaugh, for teaching me the word of God and leading me through the fiery trials of becoming a steward of the message of the gospel, and for taking the time to write the foreword of this book. It's an incredible honor.

I also have to thank my dad for demonstrating the heart of the loving Father, which this book is all about. The Lord's children discover his heart in many ways—for me, it began with my dad, Stephen Nelson: an amazing Father to 5 crazy kids. He joyfully walked alongside us as we spent our childhood reveling in the wonders of this strange world, created by a wonderful architect.

Finally, thank you, Jesus, for graciously laying down your life for me, pulling back the veil, and revealing the incomprehensible beauty of the source and sustainer of our existence, our heart's companion: ***the God of Wonders.***

## DEDICATED TO:

*Bethany, Anna, Abby, and Niklas.*
*My lifelong co-laborers in the works of wonder.*

*On the glorious splendor of your majesty,*
*and on your wondrous works, I will meditate.*

*—Psalm 145:5*

***Divine Wonder***



Published by Agápe Studios. Winona, MN 55987 USA


Published in the United States of America.

ISBN: 979-8-9889805-4-4

# CONTENTS

# FOREWORD

I first met Jon at 6 a.m. at Planet Fitness. He was the energetic blonde kid behind the front desk; I was the bleary-eyed guy trying to wake up for a workout. As he introduced himself to me, I was struck by one thing—his deep sincerity.

Over time, during those early-morning greetings, I began to hear his heart and story. He had grown up in a Christian home. He loved soccer. He had just come back from serving the Lord overseas in Ukraine. God was awakening in him a desire to serve Jesus in ministry for his life.

The more I came to know him, the more I was struck by his purity of heart. I was struck by his childlikeness.

In the gospel of John, when Jesus meets Nathanael, he exclaims, "Behold, an Israelite in whom there is no guile!" That is Jon Nelson.

That Fall, Jon enrolled at the ministry training school I lead in Kalamazoo, Michigan. Over the next 3 years, I had the privilege to watch his life up close. I was a witness to the forging of his convictions, the clarifying of his calling, and the developing of his gifting. But even as He grew, it was the utter earnestness of his heart that marked him as a leader.

When I was Jon's age, I moved to China with my best friend for a year to tell other people about Jesus. We were about as ignorant and naïve as 2 missionaries moving to a new nation could be. We didn't know the language or the culture. But as we walked onto a Chinese college campus for the first time, we discovered a generation who could speak English and was desperately looking for something to believe in. Over the next 10 months, I felt like I was living in the Book of Acts. We baptized new believers secretly in our bathtub, we saw miraculous healings, answered prayer was a daily reality, and friend after friend met Jesus. I remember vividly walking home from seeing God move, feeling like I was floating because my heart was so overflowing with wonder. I was simply in awe of how good God was and that He was using me.

But then the years pass, challenges mount, disappointments accrue, and that feeling of floating falls back to earth. That sense of wonder gets ground down by the friction of life, colors seem a little less vivid, and we make peace with a life in black and white.

Twenty years later, God used the book you hold in your hands to call me back to that child-like perspective of wonder. I pray that it awakens wonder in you as you walk through its pages.

There is something about a young man who simply takes God at his word that can awaken faith again in those of us who have been ground down by the challenges of life. There is something about a young man's simplicity of love that can help us return again to the one thing that is needed.

As you read this book, my prayer is that comparison would collapse, complexity would melt away, and a child-like simplicity and wonder would be awakened in your heart again.

*Toby Cavanaugh*
*Director, Radiant School of Ministry*

*Introduction*

# BECOME LIKE CHILDREN

They say the eyes are the window to the soul, our gaze expresses far more than words ever could; your mouth can keep secrets, but your eyes tell the truth.

I get concerned when I look in the eyes of those around me. These days, it seems like people will tell me one thing, but their eyes tell otherwise: "I'm doing great!" they say. But their eyes look fearful, tired, and conflicted, and many just look empty.

I'm twenty-two years old now. I've seen the bright gleam in the eyes of many people slowly grow dim as life begins to wear them down. The more we shift from children to adults, the more we experience unprecedented challenges, harmful relationships, betrayal, and rejection. Slowly, we grow more and more fearful and insecure. Still, each day we go through the motions, constantly looking around and measuring ourselves up to others, trying to find some sense of security—not enough.

We go home and lie down. We're overwhelmed, paralyzed by the endless list of things we need to accomplish in order to meet the standard that we hold ourselves to. So we shut off our brains, turn on our phones, and scroll through social media, rummaging through the endless stream of photos and videos that show us the best sides of everybody else. We measure ourselves up to them and we're just not enough; the vacuum of insufficiency in our heart continues to grow deeper and wider.

The more sufficient we try to become, the less sufficient we seem. We pick up more and more insecurities, and our aspirations develop far more rapidly than the means to accomplish them. We put our phones aside, sighing as we ditch the list of things we wanted to accomplish that afternoon, eat dinner, watch some TV, and fall asleep. Tomorrow we will do it again.

Somehow in this cycle we lose our ability to think outside the box, we get so comfortable trying to replicate what we see around us, that we no longer have the ability to dream or embrace our uniqueness. Instead, we identify with whatever we can to feel accepted. In doing so we transform into machines designed to accomplish whatever it is we find our worth in. We pretend like we know what we're doing enough to get a job, get married, have kids, and then teach them to do the same.

I just recently got married to my wife, Phoebe, and in this cycle of life built on systems of comparison and competition, I've already pretty much checked off one of the most exciting parts. Phoebe and I don't have any kids yet, but I get really excited when I think about having kids. Oftentimes, when I interact with children, there's something almost impressive about the look in their eyes; the things that they say are silly, but the look in their eyes is so much more confident and exciting than that of adults. Children understand the least, are capable of accomplishing the least, but somehow they're so much more secure. Somehow, they're experiencing a reality that we have been trying to strive our way back into ever since we were in their shoes. They're so hopeful, so excited!

Children carry something beautiful that they haven't been forced to get rid of yet: their imagination. They haven't yet bought into the system of comparison, teaching us to replicate the lives of those around us in fear of not being enough, so they just explore the abundance of everything that they are yet to discover. They walk around and they experience ***wonder***. ***Wonder*** is defined as ***"a feeling of surprise mingled with admiration, caused by something beautiful, unexpected, unfamiliar, or inexplicable."*** This is a state of being that is inflicted within us by an outside source.

*Wonder* is the natural human response to the nature of God; it's a state of being that we are made for, not just as children but as adults, too. We're made in the image of a creator, and we're designed to wonder and explore as God leads us to create new things. Creativity does not come unless wonder comes first. It's impossible to create anything unless we first explore the realm of all that has not yet been created.

In a book called *"Breakpoint and Beyond"*, author George Land describes a study, which was conducted by himself and Beth Jarman, assessing the creative potential of children as they age. In the assessment, they tested 1,600 children, using a NASA-developed test to study the correlation between children and creativity levels. The researchers went through this test with kids aged 4-5 years old, and found that a total of 98 percent of them scored at a "genius" level on the test. They ran the same test with the same group of kids at ages 10 and then again at 15.

The results revealed a large drop in the percentage of children still achieving that level of creativity, with only 12 percent of these kids remaining at a "genius" level by age 15. They did further testing on 280,000 adults and 2 percent of these adults had sustained the creativity levels demonstrated at 5 years old.

2 percent.

After witnessing the decline in creative ability from 5 years old to adulthood, this is what the study concluded:

*"Uncreative behavior is* ***learned."***

The majority of us are actually taught uncreative behavior as we age. We grow up in a world where we are constantly being compared with others, so naturally we learn to do the same to ourselves. Eventually comparison teaches us uncreative behavior, it convinces us we have to replicate what we see around us in order to be accepted. When we believe the narrative that this is what we have to do in order to be enough, a little bit of our imagination is stolen from us.

However the test shows us that as children, before we buy into the narrative of comparison and competition, creativity is actually produced naturally. Creativity is a by-product of our lives when we feel safe and secure with the way God had created us to be! The ability to wonder is sustained in the place of relational intimacy with our creator. Wonder always begins with directing our attention towards Him. The problem is, there's not a whole lot of ***"wonder"*** when it comes to the conversation about God in our society. The truth is we either reject him because we cannot fully comprehend Him, or, we pretend like we can.

Both are dangerous.

## Born Again

Our unwillingness to trust God will never be satisfied by trying to fully comprehend him. As children, the sense of safety and confidence a child has is never in their own sufficiency and understanding of the world around them, it's the security, the trust established in whoever has taken responsibility for caring for them. When a newborn baby first comes into the world, all they can do is trust; this is why many parents will tell you that the first couple of years raising a child should be completely devoted to establishing trust. It's because the behavior of a baby is determined by whether or not they've come to find security in their environment. That might make sense to you, but many don't realize that the same is true when you're born-again.

In order to settle into a new identity as children of God, we need to become completely devoted to growing in trust with the Father. Many people will have misconceptions of a God that they cannot trust and take those misconceptions with them into their church environments. This, along with them the mentalities of self-sufficiency and self-preservation these misconceptions produce; often go unaddressed, and then we wonder why the church can become a place of performance, fear, and competition. This happens when we grow into the practices of the faith without simultaneously growing in dependency on the Lord. God, being our father, will often draw us into situations where we have to become entirely dependent on Him, so that trust is established when He comes through. It's a strengthening and renewal of our dependency on him.

I've been wholeheartedly following the Lord for over five years now, and I'm just now beginning to have direction beyond the year I'm currently living in. I may not have understood it back then, but the last season of my life was not about establishing a career, fulfilling my calling, or doing impactful things for the kingdom, it was about establishing trust. To this day my trust in the Lord continues to be tested and strengthened. It's the most fundamental part of being in His family. I cannot receive the joy and security of being in a dependent relationship with the Lord if I do not trust him wholeheartedly. The strength of our faith is only as strong as our willingness to recognize God as worthy of being depended on. This is Jesus' reason for saying:

> ***"...unless you turn, and become like little children you will by no means enter the kingdom of heaven." —Matthew 18:3***

The command from Jesus to become like children, is a command to change the way we think, and that's exactly what it means to repent—to turn from the way that we've learned to view the world around us, and obtain a new perspective. We have to be born-again, not just in spirit, but in our way of thinking. This means learning to see the world through the lens of a child, who is adopted by the all knowing, unconditionally loving, creator of the universe, who is completely and entirely worthy of our trust.

SO IF YOU'RE WILLING TO RECEIVE THIS INVITATION TO BECOME LIKE A CHILD, TO OBTAIN A NEW WAY OF THINKING, AND RESTORE YOUR ABILITY TO LET GO. TO TRUST, DREAM, HOPE, AND WONDER, COME ALONG WITH ME AS WE SEARCH THE SCRIPTURES TO DISCOVER THE HEART OF THE FATHER WE HAVE BEEN SO GRACIOUSLY ADOPTED BY.

# 1 OVER THE WATERS

A poet named T.S. Elliot once said, *"What we call the beginning is often the end. And to make an end is to make a beginning. The end is where we start from."*

Feel free to read that again.

There's a story behind every beginning, and today we are going to start from the end—the end of the beginning.

The beginning of our existence was the end of our non-existence, which ended with a single statement; it was more than a statement, it was a declaration: *"Let there be light."* These words mark our beginning, but it was the end of another story. Here's how the story goes:

> ***"In the beginning God created the heavens and the earth. The earth was without form, and void; and darkness was on the face of the deep. And the Spirit of God was hovering over the face of the waters." —Genesis 1:1***

There are various elements to this story; we see two separate realms: *"heavens"* and *"earth."* We're told that the earth is formless and *"void."* The word for *"void "* in ancient Hebrew is *"tôû"*, which translates to *"confusion"* and *"meaninglessness."* Try to imagine a huge formless void of confusion and meaninglessness; Do you see it? Me neither.

At this point in the creation story, our *"Earth"* is currently a weird combination of nothing and everything, a meaningless and formless dimension, a blurry blob; *"Darkness"* is looming over the face of earth– darkness is an absence of light, no clarity or contrast, no order.

God is moving–

*"The Spirit of God was hovering over the face of the waters"*

But water hasn't been created yet?— If you're confused, that's understandable, me too.

The term *"waters"* is used in the passage to depict the chaotic nature of the Earth's state. Throughout the Bible, water often represents chaos and unseen realities. Do you know that only 5-10 percent of the ocean has been explored to this day? We have no idea what kinds of creatures lurk beneath the surface. Much of the world remains unexplored because it hides in the darkness, deep within the surface of the waters— frightening.

In this picture, the Spirit of God is hovering over the realm of darkness, moving over the chaos of infinite possibilities, and he's about to do something with it. In my opinion, this is one of the most beautiful pictures in all for scripture; For many reasons, it shows me that God can take the chaos of our lives, areas of our hearts and that are the most disorienting and hardest to for us to comprehend, and he resides above it all; before the Lord does anything, he looms over endless stream of possibilities, he hovers over everything that is yet to take place, and he considers ***everything.*** There is no circumstance, no idea, no dream, no possibility that escapes the mind of the Lord; his understanding is so far beyond what we have the capacity to imagine. In light of this reality, we're left with no choice but to ditch our own understanding and lean on his.

When you try to look back before anything was created, you're left with nothing but the disorienting ***infinitude*** of possible realities. This reality of chaotic meaninglessness is the *"darkness"*—the realm of disorder, where clarity does not exist, light does not exist. This is the *"darkness"* that *"covers the surface of the deep."*

To summarize, at this point in time, two separate realms are created, heavens and earth, and the earth has no form. The world is simply chaos. We're told God is moving, or *"hovering"* over the surface of the chaotic waters. A grand confrontation, the Spirit pacing, back and forth, staring into the chaos. And then suddenly, He speaks. *"Let there be light."*

As humans, when we speak, we primarily speak descriptively; I can speak and say things like: "the sun is hot" and "the sky is blue"; when God speaks, the substance of his word comes into actuality; God says *"let there be light"* and then *"light"* exists. After that, he creates two lights, a light to rule the day (the sun), and a light to rule the night (the moon). God speaks, and whatever he speaks comes into being, exactly the way he intended it.

Generally, when we, Bible-believing Christians, talk about the beginning of the universe, we describe the beginning as the moment God said *"let there be light"*, but that wasn't the case; the heavens and the Earth were created before He said those words. Likewise, the sun wasn't created the moment he said let there be light, but there's another form of light: the illumination of all meaning and truth, when chaos is put into order.

In the apostle John's account of the gospel, He writes this about Jesus:

> ***"The light shines, and the darkness can not overcome it." —John 1:5***

In the moment when God says *"let there be light"*, the pre-existence of possible realities in our universe comes to a sudden end, and the beginning begins. And Jesus, being the living word of God, was at the center of the creation story, it was by the word of God, that the world was created with meaning. And, the Bible tells us the world was created with the cross in mind:

> *"But with the precious blood of Christ, as of a lamb without blemish and without spot: Who verily was foreordained before the foundation of the world, but was manifest in these last times for you." —1 Peter 1:19-20*

Jesus is the *"light"* that shines in the darkness. What he demonstrates ultimately reveals God's intention for creating the Earth, and not only that, but reveals the heart of God to creation once in for all. In Him, the chaotic meaninglessness of our lives is replaced with purpose, meaning, and order. God takes from the infinitude of his own imagination, speaks his own heart to the chaos, and then there's order. He speaks to the darkness, and then there's light.

> *"And God saw that the light was good"*
>
> *—Genesis 1:4*

God is happy with his establishment of light. He calls it good. Then God creates the sky, the land, and the seas; he creates the plants, the sun, the moon, the stars, the creatures of the sky, the sea, and those of the land. He establishes each of these creations as *"good."* Then God created us; He gazes on His creation and He says it's *"very good."*

"Okay Jon, I get it, very interesting take on the creation story; but what does any of this have to do with becoming like children?"

I'm getting there, I promise.

In 6 days, God creates this formless void called Earth, and his imagination invades it one day at a time; But on the 7th day, God does something strange—He does nothing. He stops ***creating.*** God created us in 6 days, and then the next day he does ***nothing.***

Why does God stop? Does God need rest? Has he used up all of his supposedly ***infinite*** power and wisdom? Or, is he trying to teach us something?

I believe that the first thing that God wanted to teach us as His children was this: ***you have to know when to stop producing,*** because if you spend your whole life producing, you'll forget that ***your value is not based*** *on what you produce.* The Lord implements a strategy to remind us that our value is not based on what we have to offer. He sets apart the seventh day for rest, to remind us we have to know when to stop, because if we don't stop, we will forget that our inherent value is placed in something far deeper than our productivity.

**Reader**—we can go no further until you understand, God doesn't need anything from you; ***he wants you.*** This was God's heart from the beginning, and this is his heart today. God created you to love you; he created you so that you could experience who he is, not so you waste your life away laboring to prove your worth to him. He already assigned you worth, and guess what, this is what he calls you: ***very good.*** God created the world, and he was happy. He called it good, and then God created us; when he did, his perspective of his creation shifted. In his eyes, this world went from good to very good; this is God's word; it has to change the way we see ourselves and it has to bring clarity to the way we view God.

Author, A.W. Tozer once dropped one of the most famous phrases in church history when he wrote:

"What comes into our minds when we think about God is the most important thing about us."

There's so much truth to that! It's a frightening reality that if the things that come to our minds when we think about God aren't being shaped by the scripture He gave us, we risk the possibility of worshiping a God that doesn't even exist.

If A.W. Tozer were to walk up to me and say this phrase, I would probably say there's a lot of truth to that, but it's not just what we think about when we think about God, but equally as important, is what God thinks about when He thinks about us.

THE KEY TO FORMING A RELATIONSHIP WITH GOD IS TO DISCOVER WHAT GOD HAS SAID ABOUT US; AND THAT MEANS LETTING THIS DECLARATION SINK INTO OUR HEARTS: "VERY GOOD."

## The Soil Of Your Heart

So God creates man, out of literal dirt; and for the first time in scripture we read what many theologians call: *"inner trinitarian dialogue"* — a fancy way of saying God is talking to himself, but it's not really just talking to himself because we know that God is ***one God*** that consists of ***three persons: Father, Son, and Holy Spirit.*** I know, confusing, but remember, we're not on a journey to comprehension and control; we're on the pathway to ***wonder;*** so instead of trying to make it make sense, let's embrace the mystery of God's triune nature, because the only kind of God that can be infinitely loving is a God that has the capacity to love ***within himself.***

Anyway, he speaks to himself:

> ***"Let us make man in our image, after our likeness. And let them have dominion over the fish of the sea and over the birds of the heavens and over the livestock and over all the earth and over***

*every creeping thing that creeps on the earth." —Genesis 1:26-27*

God takes the dirt (us), and makes a man in his own image; then the passage says he breathes into his nostrils *"the breath of life"*—

*"and the man becomes a living creature."*

If you were to read this passage in its original language, you would find that the word for *"breath"* is not unfamiliar. The word is *rûah*. It means *wind, breath, and spirit*. It's the same word that is used for *"Spirit"* when it says that the *"Spirit of God was hovering over the waters."* So God takes his own Spirit, the essence of his own nature, and breathes it into us.

The breath of life is that thing that sets us apart from the rest of creation; the moment we receive the breath of life, we are welcomed into the eternal love that God has within himself. Through us, the love of God is made manifest in the Earth, through a people who are made in his own image.

But there's one thing that still might not make sense to you: Why dirt? I mean, if you're going to create the entire planet, take one creature and set that one creature apart, giving them dominion to rule and manifest the Glory of God to the world, why would you create them out of dirt? I mean, *really?* You couldn't have made us out of something cooler, like silver or gold? Here's my take: God didn't choose to make us out of gold, because when you take gold and plant a seed in it, gold does not have the capacity to do anything with that seed. But, if you take dirt, plant a seed and you cultivate it just right, the seed will take root and eventually ***produce life***. Also, it keeps us in our rightful place, dependent on the shower, and shows us what we're really worth without God's love being sown into our hearts.

With that, God gives us a command:

***"Be fruitful, and multiply, fill the earth and subdue it."***

When it comes to multiplying literally, I think we all can infer what God has told us to do here; we don't need rocket science to figure out how to multiply. However, it goes deeper. Being made out of dirt, we have within us the capacity to take something that God has instilled inside of us, and enable it to bear fruit from within us.

Allow me to share: this story begins with me at fourteen years old, sitting in the corner of my bedroom, sobbing uncontrollably. I was in terrible pain. You might think I had just experienced something horrible, like the death of someone very close to me, or maybe I'd been abused, or taken advantage of in some way; you would probably assume I must have some logical reason to be in this kind of state, but I didn't. I had nothing I could point to. My parents would ask me in a million different ways what was wrong. I didn't know what to tell them. Every day for months I would wake up feeling this pit in my stomach, so anxious I couldn't think straight. I'd get ready for school, pull myself together, and go. As the day progressed I became more and more anxious. Many days I'd be in horrible shape by the end of the day, finding myself back to the corner of my room crying.

This feeling continued for so long that my parents switched me to homeschool, I continued my education hidden away at home, and still couldn't focus. Something felt terribly wrong. For some reason, all in one moment, the weight of every burden and responsibility I would ever experience fell upon me at once. I felt like I couldn't take on all the countless responsibilities and problems that came with life in one moment, so I was helpless to do anything at all. I was paralyzed. The weight of my own existence fell upon me, and I collapsed; I caved on the inside.

My parents tried therapists, physical and mental exercises, supplements, and blood tests; nothing was helping. One night, I had a conversation with my dad; he was the best, so compassionate and willing to take time to help me try to figure out what was wrong with me. I was trying to describe the pain I was feeling and found it difficult; the frustration brought me to a breaking point. I told him I didn't want to be alive anymore, and I told my dad I wanted to take my own life.

That's a big statement, not a fun one to hear from your son. My dad responded calmly. He said something to me that I couldn't forget: ***If I respond to this feeling the way that this torture wants me to, my enemy would win the war over my life***. That was a wake-up call for me.

The conversation ended, and I found myself back on the ground in that same corner of my room crying, and I spoke to God. I said, "God *if* you're real, I need you to show up. I can't live like this anymore."

I can't tell you in that moment that the ceiling opened up, colorful light beamed through some shiny clouds, and I heard the audible voice of God tell me in perfect detail exactly how my life was going to pan out. That didn't happen. ***But I did receive something;*** a distinguishable thought suddenly invaded my imagination and took residence in my mind: "Maybe it's not all on my shoulders, maybe God has a plan."

After that moment, I was no different than I was before; I had the same fears, the same insecurities, the same attitude, and the same problems. However, from that moment on I had something within me that I didn't have before: ***a sliver of hope.*** I received a seed in the form of an invasive thought, one that contradicted every other thought and took root in the deepest places of my mind.

What took place over the following years is so much better than just simply recovering my will to live. I began to find a deep sense of security, identity, and with that I found purpose. With purpose, I found meaning, and then finally began to discover my destiny. All of those things that now give my life joy and meaning began with a divine intervention and a seed of hope.

REMEMBER, OVER TIME, IF A SEED IS CARED FOR JUST RIGHT, THE SEED WILL GROW. IN THE RIGHT CONDITION, THE SEED PLANTED IN THE DIRT WE'RE MADE FROM HAS THE ABILITY TO CREATE LIFE.

# 2 THE ABRAHAMIC ANOINTING

A couple of years ago, I was at a beautiful Christmas party for a school that I was attending through *Radiant Church* in Kalamazoo, Michigan. We had all just gotten done eating dinner, and I was sitting at a table talking to my childhood best friend Matt and his wife. I got to be the best man in their wedding just a few months before, and now I'm sitting with them, and Matt says he has something to tell me. As he said these words, Matt had a nervous, but also enthusiastic look on his face. Immediately I knew—they're pregnant. Well, his wife, Michayla was pregnant, but he looked way more nervous about it than she did.

At this time, Matt had just turned 20 years old. Matt and I grew up doing everything together, we were in the same classes, we had a bunch of similar hobbies (riding scooters, nerf wars, you know, fun kid stuff). But now Matt is being taken into an entirely different season of his life. I'm experiencing a variety of emotions: joy, excitement, maybe a little nervous for him—I couldn't even imagine being a father yet and here my best friend was, the kid I was on the playground with in elementary school, now just a few months away from being a father. I have no idea what it's like being a dad, but I felt like the Lord gave me a word for him, so I told him: "Matt, the only way you'll find peace while raising children is if you trust the Lord with them, focus on your place as his son and love those kids the way the Lord has loved you, **sonship is the key to fatherhood.**"

As I was saying that phrase, I realized the Lord spoke to him more deeply than I understood. I can imagine that raising kids takes a ton of faith, I get nervous just thinking about it, but having children is also one of the greatest opportunities to demonstrate God's heart as a father; not one to be taken lightly.

It's fascinating to me that oftentimes when God wants to bring someone closer to himself, he gives that person a promise or a command that they can't fulfill on their own. Fatherhood is no exception, but over the last couple of years, I've gotten to watch Matt flourish as his heavenly Father guides him through the journey of being a father himself. Matt is doing amazing. Recently, I had breakfast with him, dropping him off after, I was flooded with emotion as I watched him run to his wife and his daughter, while they waited for him at the door, it was like watching the end of a beautiful movie. Matt's a great dad; but what makes Matt such a great dad is his willingness to trust the Lord to be a good father to him.

## Father Abraham

In Genesis chapter 12, we're introduced to a man named Abram. The first thing we learn about Abram is that he's a descendant of Shem, son of Noah, and he has three brothers, then one passes away, then he marries a woman who's barren. His name, Abram, means *"high father, or exalted father."* The Bible doesn't say why he made the decision to marry a barren woman, or if they knew she was barren, but the Bible does hold names with great significance. When you're given a name, you're expected to live it out.

When we're introduced to Abram, we're introduced to a man who has been called *"father"*, but it's impossible for him to become one. I wonder what was going through Abram's mind when he discovered the woman he had married was barren. The Lord shows up and commands Abram to leave home, to go to a new land that the he will reveal to him, then then he gives Abram a promise:

> *"I will make you a great nation, and I will bless you and make your name great, so that you will be a blessing." —Genesis 12:2*

This is an incredible promise, the Lord prophesies a legacy over Abram that at this time, many men would want more than anything. But it doesn't really challenge Abram's faith too much. It's not specific enough. Abram has people in his household to leave his legacy with; the challenge is going to come when God calls him to be something he could never become on his own:

> *And Abram said, "Behold, you have given me no offspring, and a member of my household will be my heir." And behold, the word of the Lord came to him:*
>
> *"This man shall not be your heir; your very own son shall be your heir." And he brought him outside and said, "Look toward heaven, and number the stars, if you are able to number them." Then he said to him, "So shall your offspring be." And he believed the Lord, and he counted it to him as righteousness. —Genesis 15:3-6*

There are a few incredible things to point out about this passage. The first is: *"The word of the Lord came to Him."* Oftentimes, we as believers go around chasing a word from the Lord because we have a hard time trusting that he's willing to give us a word of His own accord. We get so obsessed with trying to earn a word for ourselves that we actually miss the word when it comes because we fail to recognize the nature of our relationship with the Lord, and how he communicates with us, we don't find him, he finds us. In this passage, we see that the word of the Lord came to Abram. He didn't have to chase it, he just had to receive it.

We also need to recognize that the Lord doesn't condemn Abram for addressing the doubt he was experiencing; Abram had a name, but he didn't have the means to fulfill it. That's a reasonable thing to be concerned about. The Lord didn't explain to him at that moment how he was going to accomplish his purposes in Abram's life, but he gave him a word of assurance, a promise:

*"Look toward heaven, and number the stars, if you can number them." Then he said to him, "So shall your offspring be."*

What a profound promise. Abram's faith is demonstrated, and the passage says:

*"He believed in the Lord, and he counted it to him as righteousness."*

It's interesting to see that righteousness is demonstrated in taking God at his word. It demonstrates how we're to respond when God invites us to partake in his promises, even if it seems unnatural. The text doesn't say that Abram immediately started building a crib, talking about baby names and looking on Facebook Marketplace for cute clothes for babies; it says *"he believed."* His righteousness was demonstrated in his way of thinking.

## Our Ishmael

The greatest challenge we face when we receive a word from the Lord is almost always in the form of a temptation to fulfill it in our own strength. The promise is always easy to believe when it's vague, because we can search for loopholes in the promise to do God's job for him when we are faced with road-blocks. This is exactly what Abraham and his wife do:

> *Now Sarai, Abram's wife, had borne him no children. She had a female Egyptian servant whose name was Hagar. And Sarai said to Abram, "Behold now, the Lord has prevented me from bearing children. Go in to my servant; it may be that I shall obtain children by her." And Abram listened to the voice of Sarai. So, after Abram had lived ten years in the land of Canaan, Sarai, Abram's wife, took Hagar the Egyptian, her servant, and gave her to Abram her husband as a wife. And he went in to Hagar, and she conceived.*
> *—Genesis 16:1-4*

In an effort to try to make good on God's promises without having to trust in him, they make the decision of using Hagar, an Egyptian servant, to make Abram a father. The plan sort of works, Ishmael is born, along with a lot of very strange family dynamics. But now Abram is living out his name, just not the way God intended. God blessed Ishmael, but his plan still remained; those to inhabit the land of Israel will come from the barren womb of his wife, Sarai.

Most of the time, God's promises are always easy to believe until they become specific. That's where God demonstrates his power the most, and where we are most given the biggest challenge in our willingness to take him at his word. The Lord shows up again, changes his name to *"Abraham"*, which means *"father of many nations."* He reveals that the promise is coming from the barren womb of his wife.

As the promise becomes more specific, the inheritance becomes greater. Oftentimes, the greatest challenges in our faith reap the greatest inheritances. It's easy for us to become so attached to our way of choosing to fulfill God's promise that we have a hard time when God reveals what his actual plans are. This was certainly the case for Abraham:

> *Then Abraham fell on his face and laughed and said to himself, "Shall a child be born to a man who is a hundred years old? Shall Sarah, who is ninety years old, bear a child?" And Abraham said to God,* ***"Oh that Ishmael might live before you!"***
> *—Genesis 17:17-18*

Ishmael represents our efforts to achieve God's promises in our own strength. The reality is those efforts can even be blessed for a time, but eventually, we are faced with the reality that it wasn't what the Lord always intended. His ways are so much higher than ours. Ishmael was loved by the Lord and blessed by him, but Abraham was forced to confront the reality that the promise was still coming. As we take steps and discover God's will in our lives, this will happen to all of us. The important thing is that we surrender our own understanding and come back under the authority of God's will once it's revealed to us. We have to be willing to let go of our Ishmael's, and hold everything with open hands.

God loves to fulfill his promises in extraordinary ways, because when we do receive what He promises to give us, it's in a posture of dependency. Everything the Lord does, he does to bring us closer to himself. The worst imaginable thing for us would be to be given our inheritance and then left to wield it on our own. When we hold onto the things that God gives us without trusting him to give us the wisdom to steward it, we become subject to all sorts of negative possibilities. This includes a fear of loss that produces self-protection, and poor stewardship that eventually just produces loss anyway. Everything he gives us has to be subject to his will.

WE HAVE TO BE WILLING TO LET GO OF OUR ISHMAELS, AND HOLD EVERYTHING WITH OPEN HANDS.

In Luke 15, Jesus tells us the story of the prodigal son: A son demands his inheritance from his father and takes off with it. He spent it all on "reckless living," lost everything, and returned home empty-handed. If you've heard the story, you know that this son is welcomed home with open arms, and it's a wonderful message about God's grace, but the message contains principles about stewarding our inheritance. If we receive our promises and keep them under the guidance of our wise and trustworthy Father, we'll do much better to get everything out of it that he has intended for us.

When Abraham is hit with the revelation that his descendants are to come from Sarah, his barren wife, he's forced to trust God to fulfill the promise on his own accord; and he has to drop his own efforts to do God's job for him.

When we're willing to trust God with the future, we're given a unique authority to wield in the present. Abraham finally lets go and stops trying to fulfill the promise on his own, so he's able to recognize what the Lord is inviting him into at that moment. The Lord reveals a coming judgement on Sodom and Gomorrah. The Lord says: *"the outcry against Sodom and Gomorrah is great and their sin is very grave."* The cities are about to be wiped out completely.

Abraham pleads the case of the righteous in those nations, and the Lord agrees that he will not destroy those who are innocent in that nation. Then it says *"the Lord went his way, when he had finished speaking to Abraham, and Abraham returned to his place."*

In this story, Abraham had been positioned to trust the Lord with his own destiny, and only then was he was able to see beyond himself and plead the case of others. This is the first demonstration of intercessory prayer that we see in the Bible. The story shows us that trusting in the will of God positions us to see beyond ourselves and plead the cause of others. This is the Abrahamic anointing; it's the anointing of faith, to dwell in the security of God's promises, so much so that we can plead the case of the innocent, having faith for those who have none. The Lord has called us to glorify him to the Earth by pleading his case and declaring his will over others as he reveals the need. I've heard it said that ***the spirit of revelation is the mantle for intercession***. The Spirit of revelation reveals the heart of God, and with it comes the responsibility to declare it over the broken and the needy.

For Abraham, the Lord continues to show himself faithful to keep his promises. Eventually, Abraham's son Isaac is born. The descendants of Isaac become a great nation, inhabiting the land of Israel, eventually becoming the lineage of Christ himself.

God has to take Abraham through an intense season of establishing trust before Abraham could father the nation of God's people. The story of Abraham is a testimony that our Father is faithful to keep his promises.

IN MOMENTS WHEN WE ARE CONFRONTED WITH OUR OWN BARRENNESS, GOD'S POWER AND WISDOM PAVE A WAY FOR US TO BECOME ALL THAT WE WE'RE MADE FOR, AND IN HIM, WE LOOK TO THE FUTURE WITH HOPE, EXPECTANCY, AND WONDER.

# 3 IDENTITY EXCHANGE

## Burning Bushes and Broken Cisterns

Our God is so creative, far more than what we have the capacity to imagine. He uses his creativity to demonstrate who He is in beautifully complex and multifaceted ways; in the words of Isaiah the prophet:

> *"Have you not known? Have you not heard? The Lord is the everlasting God, the Creator of the ends of the earth. He does not faint or grow weary; his understanding is unsearchable." —Isaiah 40:28*

We celebrate the unsearchable nature of God because it means he's a well we can drink from that never runs dry. Our God is the eternal source of all wisdom and insight. If you're bored or disinterested with God, it's not because he's boring; it's because you've become satisfied with an inferior source.

In the 1990's the soda company Sprite had a slogan: *"OBEY YOUR THIRST."* I didn't drink Sprite at the time, I wasn't born yet. I actually just saw it online, but I thought it was ironic, when you drink soda it actually does nothing for your thirst at all. It may be refreshing for a moment, but with all the sugar content, it doesn't hydrate you even a little bit; soda actually just dehydrates you. You get a feeling of temporary pleasure, but your need hasn't been met at all, It's just been hidden for a moment where it continues to grow. We live in a generation that loves to conceal our issues and act like we fixed them; you're anxious? Try weed; tired? Have a Red Bull, a Celcius, or a Venti Carmel Crunch Frappucino from Starbucks, that should help. These things all act as "bandages" that many of us use to conceal issues that need a better form of treatment to actually heal.

When I was a kid I went sledding in the backyard of my friend Matt's house (same guy from last chapter). Matt had a big hill in his backyard that went down into a pond. It was super fun to sled on, but you had to stop the sled before you got to the pond or else you'd risk going through the ice. One day, I went sledding with Matt, and as I was placing my had down to stop myself, I placed it on a sharp stick that sliced a deep hole in my hand.

Matt's mom took me home, and I showed my dad the hole. He saw the blood and went to grab some bandages, but when he got a look at it he said to me "I don't know if I can fix this one for you bud." What he meant was that slapping a couple Star Wars bandages on it wasn't gonna do the trick. He took me to the ER and I had to get like 10 stitches. The moral of the story is if my dad had stuck the bandages on it instead of taking me to ER, it wouldn't have healed. The same is true when we look to other sources to find healing in areas that can only be healed by God. This unfortunately becomes a way of life for the Abraham's descendants, and the Lord points out the error in their way of thinking:

> ***"For my people have committed two evils: they have forsaken me, the fountain of living waters, and hewed out cisterns for themselves, broken cisterns that can hold no water." —Jeremiah 2:13***

Two "evils" are addressed: The abandonment of their source of eternal nourishment, and the formation of sources of unsatisfactory nourishment that cannot sustain them or provide what they need. When we step into an identity of self-sufficiency, we create sources of counterfeit nourishment that we can control. The problem is that we're designed for one source of nourishment, God himself. And while we may be able to medicate and distract ourselves with other forms of satisfaction, we're just distracting ourselves from what we were created for. We were created to be dependent on the Lord for everything: identity, community, security, whatever you can think of.

To live in this way is to operate in our identity as sons and daughters of the living God.

Self-sufficiency always turns into slavery; we become slaves to the sources of provision that we go to when we turn away from the Lord. These sources of nourishment and identity run dry so quickly, and we're demanded to hew out another cistern, which will also be incapable of holding water. This is how drug use turns into drug addiction—you become a slave to your source of comfort.

This is exactly what happened to the descendants of Abraham, the people of Israel. A man named Joseph brought his father, Jacob, and the sons of Jacob to Egypt. They had children, and their children had children, and this went on for generations. Slowly, they became so comfortable in their place with Egypt that they neglected the promise that had been given to their father Abraham. They were eventually taken advantage of and turned into slaves in Egypt.

God had a purpose and an identity for them, but they

were living out a false identity, and living out lives that contradicted who they were created to be. But God, being a good father, sees his children living as slaves, and makes arrangements for an identity exchange. He chooses an Israelite named Moses, who's actually perfect for the role. Moses grew up in the Pharaoh's palace, so he had an idea of how to be a leader, and he was a descendant of Abraham. Moses is leading a flock of sheep, and he comes across a bush that's burning "yet it was not consumed."

At this moment, God offers Moses an opportunity for an identity exchange. God, in his creative brilliance, uses the image of a burning bush to do it. The bush that's on fire but not consumed represents many things, but for one I see God is showing Moses who he was created to be. God shows Moses a picture of his destiny: the bush is Moses, and the fire is the Lord's presence.

The destiny of Moses and the nation of Israel is that they would be a people that would dwell in the fire of God's presence, and remain unconsumed.

Our God is a God of wonders, but his wonders are never random. His creative mind demonstrates who he is and what his intentions are in beautiful ways; this time, in the form of a burning bush.

The Lord calls Moses to go to Egypt to set His people free. He promises to Moses:

> *" I will stretch out my hand and strike Egypt with all the wonders that I will do in it; after that he (Pharaoh) will let you go." —Exodus 3:20*

## Wonders in Egypt

If there's anything in the Bible that seems random, it's the ten plagues the Lord brings upon Egypt until the Israelites are set free. As I said before, our God is a God of wonders, but his wonders are never random. God is intentional; he does everything he does for a reason. He wants to set the Isrealites free, but he has a message he wants to send in the process; he is the one true God. In Egypt, they don't believe in a God, they believe in many gods. The Isrealites have been in this culture for their whole lives, so if God is going to set them free, He's gotta let them know that these other gods have nothing on him. These are the ten plagues that the Lord uses to put the god of Egpyt to shame:

**1. The Nile River turned to blood.**

There were two Egyptian gods that were exposed as inferior when Moses struck the Nile: the god *Khnum* was known as the lord of a specific section of the Nile River. *Khum* was considered the guardian of this river. The Egyptian god *Hapi* was considered the god of the annual flooding of the Nile, which would flood and dry up during the year. *Hapi* In turning the Nile to blood, the God of Israel defied both.

**2. Frogs**

A frog invasion on the people of Israel was another way of defying the Egyptian god *Heqet*. This god represented regeneration, rebirth, and fertility, Heqet was depicted as a frog-headed woman. However, this frog-god, who was supposedly almighty, could do nothing to stop an invasion of frogs and was defied by the God of Abraham.

### 3. Lice

This plague was the turning point where the magicians of Egypt gave up on trying to compete against Moses and our God. The Lord demonstrated that he could not be matched in his wonders by the work of dark magic.

### 4. Flies

The most significant aspect of this plague was that God declared that it would only affect the Egyptians, and it did. The land of Goshen, where the Israelites lived, remained untouched. This demonstrated God's power to distinguish between his people and those who opposed him. *Shu*, supposedly the god of the air and the sky, was very unhelpful for the Egyptians during this time.

### 5. Livestock Pestilence

*Hathor* was the Egyptian goddess of fertility, women, love, and the sky, was portrayed as a cow. Multiple other gods were also made in the image of livestock, such as *Amon*, who was portrayed as a ram, and *Mnevis* as a black bull. By taking Egypt's livestock in the fourth plague, the God of Israel humiliated these gods of the Egyptians.

**6. Boils**

With the plague of boils, God demonstrated His power to both wound and to heal. This didn't look good for the supposed Egyptian gods of healing, such as *Sekhmet* and *Isis*, who failed to come help out when the Egyptians had need for them.

**7. Hail**

The hail storm, described as fiery and destructive, targeted the Egyptian gods of *Nut*, God of the sky, and *Osiris*, God of agriculture, and *Set*, God of storms. The coexistence of fire and hail was a demonstration that the God of Israel was God over all forms of matter. One God in control of all. This made a mockery of the nation that constantly sought after different gods for different purposes.

**8. Locusts**

The seventh plague of Locusts was a rough one. Egyptian god *Bastet*, an idol in the form of a cat who was supposed to be the protector of crops from rodents and vermin like locusts. He wasn't helpful. Neither was *Osiris*, god of agriculture, and *Osiris* was considered the ruler of death and life, and of sprouting vegetation, and Egyptians believed that *Osiris* produced agriculture in Egypt.

### 9. Darkness

An infamous Egyptian god named *Ra* was supposedly above every other god and human in all of Egypt. In the ninth plague, God made it so dark nobody could see each other for three days...you get the point, let's move on to the last one.

### 10. Death of the Firstborn

Pharaoh lost his son in this one. It is tragic, but I have to believe that the Lord is just and righteous with all of his judgments. In Egypt, Pharaoh, and the lineage of all Pharaohs, were seen as deities, this plague was an attack on the god of Pharaoh himself. On this day, all of Egypt was confronted with a harsh reality that the Lord God was above the Pharaoh they had placed their faith in. After the final plague Pharaoh lets the

Egyptians go. What does this teach us? That God has a sense of humor, yes. But even more so, it teaches us that the ***God of the Bible*** rules above *Zeus, Budha, Ganesha, Mohammed, Dagon, Thor* (just throwing him in there), and any other "god" anyone has ever named.

## Cornered by God

God is truth, and wherever he exercises his authority, whatever is false will be confronted with the truth. In Exodus 14, the people of God are set free from Egypt; the promised land is just to the East, but the Lord does something unexpected: he sends them south. Moses is told to take the people of Israel and camp by the Red Sea.

Conveniently, at this moment, Pharaoh changes his mind, and he's not happy that he's lost all these slaves, the livestock they brought with them, and his son; he sends his Egyptian army after them, and Israel is found trapped between the greatest global military power of their day, and the Red Sea:

> *When the king of Egypt was told that the people had fled, the mind of Pharaoh and his servants was changed toward the people, and they said, "What is this we have done, that we have let Israel go from serving us?" So he made ready his chariot and took his army with him, and took six hundred chosen chariots and all the other chariots of Egypt with officers over all of them. And the Lord hardened the heart of Pharaoh of Egypt, and he pursued the people of Israel while the people of Israel were going out defiantly. The Egyptians pursued them, all Pharaoh's horses and chariots and his horsemen and his army, and overtook them encamped at the sea, by Pi-hahiroth, in front of Baal-zephon. —Exodus 14:5-9*

I've read this passage many times before. It wasn't until recently that I took my attention off of the actions of Pharaoh in this moment and started to focus on what the Lord was doing. He does all of these amazing wonders to free the Isrealites, sends them to the Red Sea, and then he actually hardens

Pharaoh's heart so that he sends the Egyptian army after them. Suddenly, the same God that freed them from Egypt positions the Israelites so that they are cornered between the raging sea and the infuriated Egyptian army. The Israelites freak out:

> *They said to Moses, "Is it because there are no graves in Egypt that you have taken us away to die in the wilderness? What have you done to us in bringing us out of Egypt? —Exodus 14:11*

Honestly, I've heard many preachers and Bible teachers ridicule the Israelites for this response, and I get it. I mean, they just saw the Lord do all of those wonders to get them out of Egypt, and now they're giving up on him? But honestly, when I read it from this perspective, their response seems valid. From their perspective. The Lord had done all these wonders in Egypt just to take them out, trap them by the red sea, and get overtaken by the Egyptians. I would be pretty confused too. But remember, God does everything for a reason. What they say next is the key to understanding why God has them in this position.

> *"Is not this what we said to you in Egypt: 'Leave us alone that we may serve the Egyptians'? For it would have been better for us to serve the Egyptians than to die in the wilderness." —Exodus 14-12*

What comes to the surface in moments of pressure reveals who we really are, and what we really believe. This is often why God corners us, to confront the lies we believe about him, and about ourselves. For the Israelites, what rose to the surface under pressure was the lie they were believing. In Genesis, the Lord had called them to be a blessing to all nations, a lineage of kings, rulers of the promised land, but they, instead of identifying with the word of God over their lives, identified with their circumstance: Egyptian slaves. Slavery had become their identity, it shaped the way they viewed themselves, and what was best for them.

Moses said to the people, ***"Fear not, stand firm, and see the salvation of the Lord, which he will work for you today. For the Egyptians whom you see today,*** *you shall never see again. The Lord will fight for you, and **you have only to be silent.**"*

A nation composed of slaves who labor tirelessly for everything they have was just told that ***someone else was going to do the work for them;*** they're only to *"be silent."*

These words must have rocked them, imagine growing up in an environment where everyone was constantly laboring tirelessly to please a plurality of gods and all the sudden you're in a life or death situation, and you have some man telling you that God is going to do the work for you.

Moses is commanded to lift up his staff, stretch his hand over the sea and divide it, so he did— in a beautiful demonstration of God's power, the sea is driven back by a strong wind, splitting the waters and creating a path of escape for the people of Israel.

Normal reasoning would think it would be a stupid idea to lift a staff and stretch your hand over the sea in a moment like this, but because it was what the Lord had spoken, it made perfect sense to Moses. The action of a man, provoked by a word from the Lord, created a way out of a life-threatening situation. I'm convinced that if Moses would have never lifted the staff and stretched out his hand, the sea would have never split. However, through obedience to the commandment of God, Moses was granted the authority to do the impossible, to overcome an impossible challenge.

The word of the Lord is constantly available to us, but when we have become accustomed to depending on our own strength, we don't look for solutions that are beyond our own capacity. The Lord is confronting this mentality of self-sufficiency in the Israelites; their complaint revealed that it was more to them than a circumstance, it was an identity they had taken on. In their bondage as slaves, they developed a way of thinking that reinforced the lie they were living, so that the idea of freedom became offensive to them.

The Lord had taken the Israelites out of Egypt, but he had a long way to go before getting Egypt out of the Israelites; they had to be taught a new way of thinking, a new way of life.

OFTEN, AN IDENTITY EXCHANGE COMES WITH A SHIFT IN PERSPECTIVE, HAS YOUR PERSPECTIVE SHIFTED TO FIT YOUR IDENTITY AS A CHILD OF GOD?

IF NOT, WHAT COULD THAT CHANGE IN YOUR WAY OF THINKING DO FOR YOUR LIFE?

EVER WONDER?

# 4 WISDOM AND WONDER

The book of Proverbs is widely known as the primary source for wisdom in the Bible; I love the book. I try to read through all 31 chapters each month, but what I've come to notice is that the more I read Proverbs, the more I recognize the realities described in it all throughout the other 65 books in the Bible. One of the realities depicted in Proverbs is a tension that exists between our pursuit of wisdom, and the temptation to become wise in our own eyes.

We're told:

> *Get wisdom; get insight; do not forget, and do not turn away from the words of my mouth. —Proverbs 4:5*

And then we're told:

> *Be not wise in your own eyes; fear the Lord, and turn away from evil. It will be healing to your flesh and refreshment to your bones. —Proverbs 3:7-8*

So, we have to get wisdom at all costs, but the second you think you're winning, you become threatened by the danger of thinking that you are now wise. Many leaders have failed at navigating this tension all throughout the Bible, even the greatest leaders, like Moses.

## Detached From Our Dependency

In Exodus 17, Moses is instructed by the Lord to strike a rock and receive water from it for the people of Israel:

God says:

> *"Behold, I will stand before you there on the rock at Horeb, and you shall strike the rock, and water shall come out of it, and the people will drink." And Moses did so, in the sight of the elders of Israel. —Exodus 17:6*

Moses does great! He's obedient, faithful, and the Lord comes through—this time.

A while later, Moses does the same thing, but this time, he's being disobedient to the Lord:

God says to Moses:

> *"Take the staff, and assemble the congregation, you and Aaron your brother, and tell the rock before their eyes to yield its water. So you shall bring water out of the rock for them and give drink to the congregation and their cattle." And Moses took the staff from before the Lord, as he commanded him. Then Moses and Aaron gathered the assembly together before the rock,*

> *and he said to them, "Hear now, you rebels: shall we bring water for you out of this rock?" And Moses lifted up his hand and struck the rock with his staff twice, and water came out abundantly, and the congregation drank, and their livestock. —Numbers 20:8-11*

Did you notice what happened? Read it again.

The Lord commanded Moses to obtain water from a rock again, but this time, He told Moses to *"tell"* the rock to yield its water; but instead of speaking to the rock Moses struck it—not once, but twice. Striking it didn't work the first time, and instead of inquiring of the Lord, Moses proceeded with what had worked for him in the past. Moses disobeyed the Lord for the second time. There are two reasons why it happened. First, Moses became too comfortable in his own strength. It's easy to misunderstand what the Lord is asking us to do if we think we already know what's best for us. But the second reason is because Moses was disconnected from the Lord's heart; he acted out in anger. Moses' mistake was met with a harsh word of correction:

> *And the Lord said to Moses and Aaron, "Because you did not believe in me, to uphold me as holy in the eyes of the people of Israel, therefore you shall not bring this assembly into the land that I have given them." These are the waters of Meribah,where the people of Israel quarreled with the Lord, and through them he showed himself holy.—Numbers 20:12-13*

In his indignation, Moses made a rash decision to follow his own instincts and he quickly reaped consequences for it. He did more than just make a simple mistake, he disqualified himself from being the one to lead the people into the promised land. Leaders always suffer consequences when they become detached from their dependency.

King Solomon, son of David, became another example of a type of failure in leadership, but in a much more subtle way. Solomon was a man of wisdom.

As a young king, the Lord appeared to Solomon in a dream and told him to ask for *anything,* Solomon was so young, he not only had the faith of a child, he actually was a child, and he simply responded:

> *O Lord my God, you have made your servant king in place of David my father, although I am but a little child. I do not know how to go out or come in. And your servant is in the midst of your people whom you have chosen, a great people, too many to be numbered or counted for multitude. Give your servant therefore an understanding mind to govern your people, that I may discern between good and evil, for who is able to govern this your great people?" —1 Kings 3:7-9*

The humility that Solomon had in this moment was exactly what we need to be able to wield the gift of wisdom. He recognized he needed support that was beyond himself to lead the nation. The Lord responded, and Solomon was given a wise and discerning mind. Self-sufficiency and wisdom do not go hand in hand; to pick one way of life up, you have to put the other down.

## The Age of Influence

Every generation has had it's influencers, but Gen Z is the first generation that's almost entirely composed of them. We base so much of our worth on the level of influence we have that we're not even sure what we want to do with the influence when we get it, we just want it.

We're the first generation of Christians that forgets to spend time with the Lord because we're too busy trying to tell others how to do it. I see so many people abandon the church because they either aren't given a place to lead, or they're forced to wait. We use social media to dodge the process of growing in leadership within the church because we're convinced that if we don't have any influence now, we don't have worth; It's a total lie. The interesting thing is we are actually seeing so many people come to the Lord because of all of this content about God that's being thrown up on social media, and that is beautiful, but, just because you got water to come from a rock doesn't mean you're doing it the way the Lord asked you to.

I believe the most powerful days of God's church are yet to come, and it's not gonna come from a bunch of 19 year olds posting about theology on Instagram, it's gonna come from the beautiful expression of God's power from a generation of children who depend on God like they're children.

For many, social media is a mission field that the Lord has called them to, but for many others, it's a distraction from the process of growing in the knowledge of God and learning about the purpose of influence while we grow in it. If you're in Gen Z and you can't spend time with the Lord without throwing a picture of your Bible, notebook, and a pumpkin spice latte up on a Instagram; you don't influence, you need to be hidden in Christ.

Often, we seek influence because it comes with power, and power gives us control. We seek control because we don't trust God to take care of us. Solomon was given influence and the first thing he did was put God in control, he had no idea what to do with his influence, he just knew that if God told him what to do, he'd be okay. And it was, it was better than okay. During the rule of Solomon, the nation had peace beyond what they had experienced since they first became a kingdom, they flourished so much economically that the text says ***silver was worth as much as rocks***. The wisdom of God gave Solomon the decision-making skills to create a nation more beautiful and successful than anything the world had ever seen.

## The Value of Wisdom

Being a Gen Z kid, I grew up playing sports and video games, I didn't do a whole lot of reading until I graduated high school, and I never came to recognize the value of wisdom until I became older. When I thought of wisdom, I thought of super old movie characters like Master Yoda from *Star Wars,* or Master Oogway from *Kung-fu Panda;* I loved the characters but the wisdom they portrayed wasn't something that I necessarily valued in my own life.

The truth is that the pursuit of wisdom is an essential and intimate part of the way we live our lives unto the Lord. ***Wisdom*** is one word that encapsulates the mind of God being revealed to us in order to know him on a deeper level and accomplish his will, it's both beautiful and practical. Wisdom takes our faith, what we know about the Lord, ourselves, and the world around us, and applies that faith to a circumstance in an intentional way. Wisdom only functions in our lives the way it's meant to if the mind is submitted to the will of God.

> *"The fear of the Lord is the beginning of wisdom, and the knowledge of the Holy One is insight."*
> *—Proverbs 9:10*

I love this verse, wisdom only bears fruit in our lives if it is built on the foundation of obedience and surrender. So this *fear*, or reverence, for the Lord which is the beginning of wisdom isn't something that drives us away from him, but it actually draws us closer to him. The recognition of who God is enlightens us to the reality that we cannot possibly live a meaningful life without his guidance. All true insight is found in our knowledge or understanding of the Holy One. His perspective and his nature is the only thing that enables us to make sense of the world around us.

Proverbs 9:10, (the previous passage), is not the only time that this statement appears in the Proverbs, this phrase: the "***fear of the Lord is the beginning of wisdom",*** is written in Proverbs 1 as well, but King Solomon actually got the phrase from his father's Psalm, in Psalm 111. The Psalm is widely believed to be written by his father King David. It's beautiful to me because when Solomon writes his Proverbs, He writes them to his own son, the grandson of David. Wisdom is meant to be passed down through generations, and it's accessible to all who are called children of God because he identifies himself as our father.

Psalm 111, is a Psalm of praise that exalts God for His faithfulness, provision, and the beauty of his works. It's an ***acrostic*** poem, which means that each line begins with a letter of the alphabet, in alphabetical order. After the opening "Praise the Lord!" The first letter of each line is a Hebrew letter in the order of the Hebrew alphabet. Sadly, Hebrew acrostic poems are just about impossible to translate over to English, so the poetic detail is missing in all our English translations of the Bible.

Psalm 111 ends with this phrase:

> *"The fear of the Lord is the beginning of wisdom; all those who practice it have a good understanding. His praise endures forever!" —Psalm 111:10*

You know you have ***good understanding*** when you're able to actually ***practice*** the fear of the Lord, and point to it. You know that you intimately know the Lord and trust him, when that knowledge changes the way you understand the world around you, and consequentially, the way you behave as well.

The creative nature of the Psalm speaks to the essence of wisdom itself in multiple ways. The Psalm brings glory to God, and it has a creative, artistic style to it. It's wisdom and beauty.

I'm sad to say I live in a generation that sees wisdom as boring and stoic, it's not. Wisdom is beautiful, it produces creativity and excellence, and those who receive it demonstrate those two things. Wisdom can manifest itself in the form of poetry, like King David, or solutions to difficult problems, like it did with Solomon. It's manifested in art, business, sports, teachings, evangelism, academics, architecture, agriculture and more! The list can literally go on forever because there is an infinitude of expressions that the Lord is able to display in our lives if we are willing to tap into the wisdom that we find under his Lordship. Again, Godly wisdom takes our faith and makes it specific and practical.

I've heard it said by Pastor Bill Johnson, a pastor in California who has taught me so much over the years (He has no idea who I am):

*"Wisdom is like the banks of a river because it gives faith a direction to flow."*

It's a beautiful picture, but a biblical statement too.

One of my favorite Proverbs is Proverbs 21:1. I don't need to open my Bible to write it down, I've reflected on it so much throughout the last couple years I could never forget it:

> *"The king's heart is like a river in the hand of the Lord, he turns it where he wills." — Proverbs 21:1*

The thing about a river is that regardless of which way the river is turned, ***the flow remains constant.*** We are a people who are called to take initiative out of love and adoration for the Lord, and then allow His grace to influence the direction of our flow. That really is our inheritance, to see the Lord glorify himself through our works. The challenge is handling it appropriately when he steers us.

I had a really hard time when I was steered by the Lord early on in my journey of faith. Of course I didn't realize why it was happening, so I battled against it. For example, I was so committed to being a pro soccer player when I was younger; I felt like if I couldn't do it I was somehow a failure. But, it never worked out for me, and after high school I was called to the mission field. I went to Ukraine for a while, fell in love with the Lord there, and then he called me home right before the war began with Russia. When I came back I immediately began coaching soccer to try to somehow help others do what I felt like I had failed to because I never saw that the Lord was steering me elsewhere. I became so devoted to my own vision and direction that I was hurt when he tried to steer my life.

Proverbs 13:12 says ***"Hope deferred makes the heart sick, but a desire fulfilled is a tree of life."*** When we are met with disappointment, our hearts are subject to a level of vulnerability. That's what it means to be sick; sickness is a state of vulnerability, not calamity. Disappointment is not the end, it's a sign you are being steered in another direction. When hope is deferred we are vulnerable, and it's important what decisions we make in seasons of vulnerability, because if it's not handled well, it actually can result in calamity. For all my younger people *calamity* means *death*. I've seen many people become offended during a season where they are flowing passionately and the Lord steers them. The cracks in their foundation of trust with him cause them to collapse, and instead of seeing where it goes, they just stop flowing.

## The Tree of life

The latter phrase of the Proverbs 13:12 can also be translated this way: *"the desire realized is a tree of life."*

The tree of life is mentioned in 3 books of the Bible: Genesis, Proverbs, and Revelation. The 3 books listed speak respectively to all of time: past, present and future—the past in Genesis, the present in Proverbs, and the future in Revelation. In each of these time periods, the tree of life marks us in a way. In Genesis, we are separated from the tree of life and marked with our condition of sin, in Revelation we are marked with our final reunion with Christ. But in Proverbs it says we are marked with *"the desire realized."*

> ***Hope deferred makes the heart sick, but the desire realized is a tree of life. —Proverbs 13:12***

We're met with disappointment, saddened by the bitter end of our own ambitions, or even just facing the symptoms of brokenness in the world we live in. ***But,*** every disappointment is an opportunity to have our understanding enlightened by the restorative nature of the Lord's will for us. He shows us that his way is better. Being steered is inevitable when we come under the Lordship of Christ. We need His Lordship because His way is so much better than ours.

We have to be steered inwardly as we are steered outwardly, or we'll never reconcile the difference between our expectations and the outcome. This is why Jesus said *"Repent, for the kingdom is at hand."* Jesus is saying we have to change the way we think ***because*** when our desires are transformed according to his will, we actually discover that the things we hope for are actually ***at hand,*** or within reach. We're transformed by the renewing of our mind, because:

> *"...Then you will be able to test and approve what God's will is—his good, pleasing and perfect will."*
> *—Romans 12:2 (NIV)*

To walk in wisdom isn't to know the answer to every problem and never be caught by surprise. Wisdom is revealed by how we respond when things don't go the way we anticipate them to, to enable negative experiences to lead you into a greater revelation of who your Father is, and how he thinks.

WISDOM IS A CHILD'S INHERITANCE; ASK FOR IT! JUST DON'T BE SURPRISED WHEN YOU'RE TAKEN TO PLACES BEYOND WHAT YOU CURRENTLY HAVE THE ABILITY TO RATIONALIZE, THAT'S WHERE THE MAGIC HAPPENS.

*Divine Wonder*

# 5 PURCHASING PEACE

King Solomon was the wisest king the world had ever seen during his rule. He walked gracefully in the wisdom of God, using his profound insight to establish peace within his kingdom first, and then with the nations around him. His confidence as a king grew as he overcame impossible challenges with ease, and as time progressed, Solomon had an endless list of opportunities fighting for his attention. The wealthiest rulers in the world wanted to meet him and make alliances with him. Unfortunately, Solomon didn't count the cost of saying yes to all these new opportunities. Solomon sacrificed his commitment to the Lord, possibly without even realizing it, and redirected his attention to managing all he was given.

Often instead of recognizing that the Lord has answered our prayers, we become burdened with all of the things we didn't realize we were asking for when we prayed. So, instead of allowing that answered prayer to produce a greater level of trust with the Lord, and ask him what to do with everything we've been given, we try to maintain all of the responsibilities and opportunities we now have through his provision in our own strength. This is exactly what happened to Solomon. His time in the Lord's temple was superseded with visitations to other kingdoms, where he busied himself making alliances and treaties with neighboring kingdoms; often by marriage treaties, where he would marry a daughter of another ruler as a covenant of peace and unity between the two nations. He married many wives from many different nations, 700 of them.

Yep, you read that right, 700.

The house of Solomon grew, his kingdom flourished, and when rulers of other nations like the Queen of

Sheba visited, they were left breathless by the beauty of his kingdom. He was doing good, he finally had everything all under control.

*And that was the problem.*

All was well, until his disconnection with the Lord finally caught up with him. Solomon developed habits of selling his commitment to the Lord to buy peace with the environment around him. He laid down his commitment not to marry foreign women to buy peace with neighboring nations. He laid aside his commitment to honor the Lord with His authority to show respect for nations that worshipped other idols.

Eventually, the many lovers King Solomon brought into his household brought with them all the idols they worshipped. The house of Solomon became a house of not one God, but many. First, King Solomon tolerated false gods, then he accommodated for them, and eventually he began to worship them.

The wisest king the world had ever seen betrayed his source of wisdom because he had become comfortable on his own two feet, Solomon no longer recognized his need for God.

## A Bad Bargain

When the enemy wants to take control of our life, he often starts by slowly luring us out of our place of dependency on the Lord, and onto ourselves. His favorite tool is fear. I believe the enemy used fear to persuade Solomon the kingdom was going to fall apart if he didn't make marriage treaties with princesses from other lands. I'm sure the enemy manufactured lies, saying that if Solomon didn't accommodate their false gods, the peace he had established would be short-lived. Sadly Solomon bought the narrative. Years later the kingdom of Israel was split in two, as a consequence of the idolatry that began with him.

DIVISION ALWAYS MAKES A KINGDOM VULNERABLE; BUT IT ALSO MAKES A PERSON VULNERABLE. IF YOU DO ONE THING AS IF YOU BELIEVE IN GOD, BUT DO ANOTHER AS IF YOU DON'T, THE ENEMY WILL TAKE ADVANTAGE OF YOUR COMPROMISE AND DO WHATEVER HE CAN TO TEAR YOUR LIFE APART. THE ENEMY ALWAYS SEES DIVISION AS VULNERABILITY, WHETHER IT'S IN YOUR VALUES, YOUR FAMILY, YOUR COMMUNITY, OR YOUR NATION.

Several generations after the rule of Solomon, the nation Israel found themselves split into two kingdoms, the northern kingdom was Samaria, and the southern was Judah. Their differences in commitment to the Lord eventually caused a split, and the split made them vulnerable. The division made them an appealing target for neighboring nations; the north side, Samaria was conquered by the land of Assyria. The king of the south, Hezekiah, who ruled in Judah, was a descendant of Solomon. He loved the Lord zealously, and fought back against the worship of false gods in his land, tearing down idols and turning his nation back to the one true God. God's favor was on him; wherever Hezekiah went, he prospered.

Eventually the north kingdom, Samaria, was overtaken by Assyria. When Hezekiah got word of it, a seed of fear was planted in his heart. Eventually Assyria went up against the fortified cities of Judah and took them. Hezekiah's response reflected the fear in his heart, see here:

*And Hezekiah, king of Judah sent to the king of*

> *Assyria at Lachish, saying, "I have done wrong; withdraw from me. Whatever you impose on me I will bear." And the king of Assyria required of Hezekiah king of Judah three hundred talents of silver and thirty talents of gold. And Hezekiah gave him all the silver that was found in the house of the Lord and in the treasuries of the king's house. At that time Hezekiah stripped the gold from the doors of the temple of the Lord and from the doorposts that Hezekiah king of Judah had overlaid and gave it to the king of Assyria. —2 Kings 18:15-17*

Hezekiah immediately surrendered the treasures he had laid up in the Lord's temple. Instead of inquiring of the Lord, he gave into the temptation to sell what he had committed to God, and attempted to buy peace with the world around him. When we don't build habits of inquiring of the Lord in our times of need, the problems we face often seem bigger than he is. That's never actually true, but the tactic of the enemy is to convince us that it is.

Once the enemy takes from us what belongs to the Lord, he tries to take over our lives completely, and the attempt of Assyria reflects his tactics. Hezekiah came back though, when Assyria came up against Jerusalem, and Hezekiah found the courage to stand up to them, he stopped following their orders, and as the enemy often does, Assyria tried to use people around him. The Assyrian king said to the people of Judah:

> *Thus says the king: 'Do not let Hezekiah deceive you, for he will not be able to deliver you out of my hand. Do not let Hezekiah make you trust in the Lord by saying, The Lord will surely deliver us, and this city will not be given into the hand of the king of Assyria.' Do not listen to Hezekiah, for thus says the king of Assyria: 'Make your peace with me and come out to me. Then each one of you will eat of his own vine, and each one of his own fig tree, and each one of you will drink the water of his own cistern, until I come and take you away to a land like your own land, a land of grain and wine, a land of bread and vineyards, a*

> *land of olive trees and honey, that you may live, and not die. And do not listen to Hezekiah when he misleads you by saying, "The Lord will deliver us." —2 Kings 18:29-32*

The response of the people of Judah in this moment is beautiful; they were silent and did not respond a word for the king's command was "do not answer him." I can tell Hezekiah was a great leader because of this moment. The people of Judah saw him as a secure leader because he placed his trust in the Lord.

THE FIGHT IS ALWAYS FOR OUR TRUST, THE ENEMY FIGHTS TO GET US TO PLACE OUR TRUST ELSEWHERE, BUT AS CHILDREN OF GOD, OUR TRUST MUST REMAIN IN THE LORD.

## Perfect Peace

> *When the servants of King Hezekiah came to Isaiah, Isaiah said to them, "Say to your master, 'Thus says the Lord: Do not be afraid because of the words that you have heard, with which the servants of the king of Assyria have reviled me. Behold, I will put a spirit in him, so that he shall hear a rumor and return to his own land, and I will make him fall by the sword in his own land.'"*
> *— 2 Kings 19:6-7*

In this instance, Hezekiah gets it right; he sends his servants to inquire of the Lord by the prophet Isaiah, and they come back with a promise of deliverance. You are not a child of God unless his word directly impacts the way you live your life. You are only at peace as much as you are willing to trust the Lord. When I was a kid, I loved going to the beach, my siblings and I would have so much fun playing in the waves, climbing dunes, building sandcastles, digging massive holes in the sand for no reason, stuff like that. When my dad told us we were going to the beach, that meant we were going. It was about an hour away so would leave pretty early in the morning to get there when it wasn't crowded, so if my dad said we were going, that meant I had to get my swimsuit, goggles, shovel, football, and whatever I wanted to have ready the night before, and go to bed early. My actions changed because of what my dad had spoken; I didn't know how to get there, where we were stopping on the way, but I did what I could to get ready, because I knew we were going to the beach.

God is looking for people who will be stewards of his word. When God speaks, we have to adjust our lives accordingly in order to do well with the word he's spoken. The enemy will almost always offer us opportunities to compromise our trust when the Lord God speaks.

Often we become more concerned with what the enemy is saying and sell our trust with God to buy peace with the enemy; this can look like lying our way out of a mess we get ourselves into, compromising financial obedience to save money, establishing control in our environments through manipulation, you name it. The enemy is only able to accomplish his will in our lives through areas where we don't trust the Lord. Obedience is always an issue of trust; wherever we struggle to obey the Lord and commit ourselves to him, there's an underlying trust issue.

The temptation to buy peace is always rooted in a lie that peace is not already accessible to you. In Isaiah 26:3 the prophet states: *"You keep him in perfect peace whose mind is stayed on you because he trusts in you."* The condition for perfect peace is that we trust the Lord, and we know we trust him because we acknowledge him in everything we do. He's constantly on the forefront of our minds because our attention is naturally directed to whatever it is that gives us security.

I've learned to recognize seasons where I'm struggling to trust the Lord, because I could be at church, singing songs about God, and my mind will be fixed on something completely different; I'll be singing along as I obsess over issues I'm dealing with in my life, repeating scenarios, trying to come up with solutions to various challenges, worrying about who's around me, doing whatever I can to try to make myself feel productive in that moment because while I'm singing songs about how I trust the Lord, I'm trying to establish peace in my own strength. This might seem like such a small thing, but to me it's a warning signal that I'm trying to obtain a counterfeit peace.

## Prince of Peace

When Isaiah prophesied about the coming of the Messiah in Isaiah 9, one of the descriptions he gave about this person was a series of names: two of which are *"Wonderful counselor"*, and *"Prince of Peace"* he said that *"the government shall be on his shoulder"*. This is a word about a man who's an advisor and will carry a unique level of authority and establish peace wherever he rules. Counselors establish peace within us, princes establish peace around us. Isaiah says that *"of the increase of his government and of peace there will be no end."* Problems come up for believers when we believe the lie that we have gotten everything we can from God and we need to figure the rest out ourselves, but the verse says there's an unending conquest of peace that the Messiah will have. There's always a greater measure of peace that's attainable to us in him; Not comfort, but peace.

In case you haven't caught up yet, this Wonderful Counselor and Prince of Peace that Isaiah spoke of is Jesus. Paul writes in his letter to the Church of Philippi:

> *"Do not be anxious about anything, but in everything by prayer and supplication with thanksgiving let your requests be made known to God. And the peace of God, which surpasses all understanding, will guard your hearts and your minds in Christ Jesus." — Phillipians 4: 6*

Christ Jesus is the Prince of Peace, wherever he rules, he establishes peace. We're told not to be anxious but to rather be prayerful, and thankful, Paul says in this posture let your requests be made known to God.

It doesn't promise all of your requests will be granted, it promises a peace that surpasses our understanding. You know who has peace that surpases understanding?

Children.

Children don't know anything, at all, but most of the time they're at peace. As adults we behave as if the more we attain, and come to understand the world around us, the more we'll be at peace. The opposite is true, the more we come to understand, the more we are confronted with our need for God; and the more we discover the world around us, the more threatening we discover it to be. In those moments we really need to know that God is good, and he's in control. It seems so simple, but the enemy is constantly warring against these two truths, because if we know those two things in our heart of hearts, obedience and surrender become logical for us.

Obstacles appear larger than they are when we're not aware of the greatness of our God, but when we fix our attention on him, we're invited to attain new levels of faith. Peace that surpasses understanding is only as available as much as we are willing to give up our right to understand.

WHEN THE ENEMY UTILIZES FEAR IN OUR LIVES TO PERSUADE US TO SELL OUR DEVOTION TO THE LORD, AND BUY A COUNTERFEIT PEACE, WE CAN RESIST, KNOWING FULL WELL PEACE WAS BOUGHT FOR US, ONCE AND FOR ALL WITH THE BLOOD OF CHRIST.

# 6 AT THE FEET OF TRUTH

It seems like our generation has come to draw a line between faith and truth. Many of us see faith as an intangible, distant reality that doesn't actually affect much of the world around us. That's essentially more of a guess than anything else, we have no confidence in what we say we believe, so it doesn't change the way we live our lives.

Contrary to popular belief, if you're growing in faith, it does not mean you're rejecting the truth. It actually means the opposite, you grow in faith as truth becomes illuminated in your life. As children of God, we're meant to desire truth as much as we desire to grow in our faith; I believe it's God's will that we would grow in our understanding of what truth actually is as our faith expands.

Our invitation from Jesus to become like children, is not an invitation to become ignorant of truth, or to ditch our responsibility to grow in understanding; It's a call to come explore a greater reality that is far more real, and far more sustainable than what we know to be true in our own lives.

Our knowledge of the truth is always being refined, our perspectives, opinions, and desires are ever-changing. You won't be the same person five years from now that you are today, and you won't think the same, at least I'd hope not. We're destined to change, we should, we are not perfect the way we are today; but God is, and He's always the same, so we can have confidence that whatever change he brings to our lives and our way of thinking is actually good for us.

Truth is not subjective. You cannot *"live your truth"* —you're either embracing the one and only truth or you're believing a lie. Today we live in an era known as the *"me"* era, where life is all about discovering who we are. The highest calling is to *"be yourself"* to *"live your truth"*, to figure out what makes you happy and do it, no matter the cost. This is a form of worship, but the subject of our worship is the idol of self. Everyone worships something, and that something is whatever we come to place our trust in.

SELF-SUFFICIENCY TEACHES US TO BECOME OUR OWN GOD; THAT WE DECIDE WHAT IS GOOD AND EVIL, AND WE DECIDE WHAT IS TRUE.

In a culture of self-sufficiency, everything outside of our own understanding is a threat. When there's nothing outside of ourselves that we can look to for security, we have no choice but to make ourselves judge of all that is good and evil. So we decide what truth is, and in doing so we make ourselves god. Of course anxiety has increased in a culture where this is normalized, because guess what? ***You don't make a good god,*** you actually make a very bad god, and if you're the god of your life, you should absolutely be anxious, you have no idea what you're doing.

The most sustainable truths we come to understand aren't truths we discover ourselves, it's what we discover about God, because He never changes. All true peace is anchored in his unchanging nature. So I really do believe that our faith in him is the threshold to the ultimate truth.

Hebrews describes faith this way:

> *Now faith is the assurance of things hoped for, the conviction of things not seen. For by it the*

> *people of old received their commendation. By faith we understand that the universe was created by the word of God, so that what is seen was not made out of things that are visible. —Hebrews 11:1-3*

By faith we understand that the universe was created by the *word* of God. If you're willing to surrender to it, the gospel actually co-labors with the independent mind, if you are genuinely willing to pursue the truth at all costs, without compromise, eventually you will find yourself at the feet of Jesus because *truth* isn't a concept, *it's a person;* and that *person* is the *word* of God, by which the universe is created and sustained. All meaning and all truth that the universe contains is found in *him*. Our understanding of what is true grows in proportion to our intimacy with the Lord because he actually wants us to discover what is true:

> *"Behold, you delight in truth, in the inward being" —Psalm 51:6*

Many of us live under the assumption that God wants to keep us in the dark about things, He doesn't. Oftentimes the Lord will hide truths in different places to be discovered as we walk through life with him, but it is always his will that we come to greater levels of understanding as we walk alongside him. God does not see us as pawns for accomplishing his will, he invites us to be partakers in his mission on the Earth; to worship in ***spirit***, and ***truth***. Jesus says in John 15:15:

> ***No longer do I call you servants, for the servant does not know what the master is doing; but I have called you friends, for all that I have heard from my father I have made known to you. —John 15:15***

It's foolish to assume that God will just do whatever he wants on his own, he shows his will to us so that we know what to fight for. The words of God don't just give us a mission but they give us meaning, they give us life. When Jesus is introduced at the very beginning of John, he is introduced as the *"Logos"*.

This is a Greek word that really just translates to *"word"*, but its meaning goes far deeper in its context. *"Logos"* is also culturally used to describe the essence of truth that binds the world together, the perfect revelation of its creator, and that logos made flesh, is Jesus; when Jesus is being described as the *"Word"* or *"Logos"* in John 1, he is being described as the manifestation of the perfect will of God in bodily flesh. Jesus is perfect theology, in him we discover who God actually is. He is that word, which the universe was spoken into existence by. He's the manifestation of the Father, and we come to know the Father through Jesus.

Jesus is also:

> ***"The light shines in the darkness, and the darkness has not overcome it." —John 1:5***

Jesus gives us vision, clarity to make sense of the world around us; he illuminates our purpose, our calling, and our destiny. Almost every religion in the world recognizes Jesus as a good teacher, but the misconception that many have is Jesus is not just a good teacher of truthful principles, but within his identity he contains truth itself, or I should say ***himself.***

Just about anyone with a head on their shoulders can detect some form of moral value from Jesus' teachings, but you don't find life in his words until you come to recognize that Jesus himself is the author of life. I have seen way too many people take the teachings of Jesus, and submit them to their own understanding, but a god that checks off all the boxes of your own understanding is a god made in your image, not the other wary around. The teachings of Jesus are designed to conform us into his image, and in doing so bring us closer to himself, because our eternal destiny really is to know him, and have a relationship with him. (John 17:3)

When I read the gospels, one of the most unsettling realities is that in the time period when the feet of Jesus actually walked the Earth, everyone was awaiting his arrival. The Jewish people were all waiting for the coming of a promised savior, a *"Messiah"*, but when Jesus showed up, he contradicted so many ideas of this *"Messiah"* the Jewish people had made up in their heads that hardly anybody actually recognized him when he came; and even of those who he did reveal himself to, almost none of them understood what he was doing, but one person did.

## Mary of Bethany

Jesus experienced a lot of rejection during his ministry. His teachings, healings, deliverances, provisions, and wonders were never enough to satisfy the hearts of those who rejected him. Jesus was was rejected in Nazareth, his own hometown; as well as the nearby Galilean cities of Chorazin, Bethsaida, and Capernaum. It's interesting that Jesus was rejected in the places that were too familiar with him. But that's another book; there was one place he went where he was received; the town of Bethany.

Bethany is known in the Bible as the hometown of a few key figures who loved Jesus zealously; these people devoted themselves to him wholeheartedly.

The town of Bethany in the gospels is a beautiful representation of what takes place in a town where Jesus is received with open arms. At Bethany, we see the comfort of Jesus in times of sorrow, the dead come back to life, beautiful demonstrations of sacrificial worship, and fellowship with Jesus. When Jesus enters Jerusalem in his *"triumphal entry",* he comes from the town of Bethany. Even today, the Lord often begins by moving from places where He is received, he's looking for dwelling places on the Earth, where he can move from. A God who is everywhere, wants to be somewhere; he's looking for places who are willing to receive him, in the gospels, that was Bethany.

My older sister is actually named Bethany, I asked my parents why they gave her the name, my dad simply responded:

*"It was the place that Jesus loved to be."*

Pretty cool.

In Luke 10, Jesus enters this town, Bethany, and he's welcomed into the home of a woman named Martha. Then we meet her sister, Mary—a key figure of the gospels; the most interesting thing about her is that she's always found at the feet of Jesus, most notably in this passage:

> *Now as they went on their way, Jesus entered a village. And a woman named Martha welcomed him into her house. And she had a sister called Mary, who sat at the Lord's feet and listened to his teaching. But Martha was distracted with much serving. And she went up to him and said, "Lord, do you not care that my sister has left me to serve alone? Tell her then to help me." But the Lord answered her, "Martha, Martha, you are anxious and troubled about many things, but one thing is necessary. Mary has chosen the good portion, which will not be taken away from her."*
> *—Luke 10:38-42*

Imagine you're in the room with the man that everyone in your community has been crying out for your whole life, your lineage has been awaiting one man for generations and generations, and now he's in your home.

Where do you find yourself? What do you do? Are you running around trying to make your place look nice for him? Prepping your best dish for dinner? Are you working to get on his good side, hoping that you'll find favor with him? Martha did everything she could to care for him, I mean, after all, the Messiah was in her home, she didn't want to end up on the wrong side of history. Mary wasn't worried about any of that, she wanted to hear what this man had to say.

Mary was found sitting, at his feet, just listening intently, she recognized that he hadn't come to be served but to serve himself. Mary resolved that she didn't need to amuse him or entertain him. Absolutely everything that took place in this moment was for Jesus to decide, the agenda was entirely his. In humility, Mary recognized that she had nothing to offer Jesus, she was only to receive with a joyful heart. If there is one demonstration in the Bible of someone practicing what it looks like to ***become like a child,*** this was ***it.*** In Mary's eyes, Jesus had not only become the ruler of the house the moment he stepped in, he ruled over every part of her inner being.

Martha Kilpatrick, wrote in her book *"Adoration":*

*"One who sits at his feet has crowned him, and enjoys the unseen kingdom of his absolute reign and supreme protection. Our ministry to him must always begin, must daily begin at his feet. In absolute surrender."*

When Jesus walks in the room, some people receive his kingdom, others don't. Mary came before him like a child, she had nothing to offer him, she came with no agenda, no preconceived notions about his intentions; she was completely submitted and surrendered to his purposes—***this is how we sit at the feet of truth.***

Martha was found indignant, distant, laboring to earn what was already available to her; she missed the good portion because she didn't recognize ***who***

***it was that was in the room with her.*** Unknowingly, in her efforts to earn his approval, she rejected that which Jesus already had for her. Martha saw his love as transactional:

*"Martha bustled to fix his lunch and make Him comfortable; she chose to relate to his humanity; Martha would feed him. Mary stood herself in homage before him; she chose to relate to his divinity. Mary would feed on him."*

Are you spending your life laboring to feed him, or are you feeding on him?

## Many Things

> ***..."Martha, Martha, you are anxious and troubled about many things, but one thing is necessary."***
> *— Luke 10:41-42*

When we're operating outside of our identity as children of God, we become anxious and troubled about many things; the endless list of all the things we must do to become sufficient for ourselves burdens us with immeasurable weight. The infinitude of insufficiencies is unbearable because the void we try to fill can only be filled by the God of infinite wisdom, wealth, power, and love. We do not make good gods.

You can tell when a culture is infected by the narrative of self-sufficiency because it produces anxiety first, and then hopelessness. In proportion to post-christianization, suicide rates in our society have skyrocketed. What is there to hope in when all hope is placed in your own sufficiency?

I've experienced this personally. When I fell into the abyss of depression in high school, it was because I was unable, or unwilling to anchor my hope in the realm of the unknown, and lean on God. My culture had taught me to become the god of my own life, so I had no place to find hope outside of myself. I became detached and suicidal when I couldn't ignore the fact as long as it was all up to me, I was inching towards an impending doom. Some people manage to ignore this reality by excusing themselves away:

*"I'll figure it out, I always have."*

But, hidden deep within their delusion, their hearts search for the meaning behind the things they do; trying to make sense of their idolatry. Meanwhile they place their hope in the next drink, the next hit, the next hook up, the next accomplishment, always anxious and troubled about many things—

*"but one thing is necessary."*

What I'm not advocating for is Cultural Christianity. Martha's actions are the way that many Christians live their lives in our society: always working to earn the approval of the Lord, accusing others that don't do such. These people have been desensitized to the gospel and many of them do not understand it's nature.

I recently heard our President Donald Trump say his efforts to establish peace between Ukraine and Russia were so that he might earn his way to heaven, saying: *"I wanna try and get to heaven if possible.*

*I'm hearing I'm not doing well. I am really at the bottom of the totem pole. But if I can get to heaven, this will be one of the reasons."*

I mean no dishonor to the President, it's possible he was only saying this to communicate that his efforts were meant to be honoring to the Lord, but regardless I want to highlight the language, oftentimes, when Christian practices become culturized, we develop a mentality that we do things ***for*** our faith, rather than ***from*** our faith. So many people see salvation as a wage for our dues, glorifying the works of man and neglecting the gift of God. To receive salvation from Christ is to sit at his feet and receive the gift of his intervention in our lives. It's really a beautiful picture.

## Worship and Wonder

To sit at the feet of Jesus is to give to him a hearing ear; one who is distracted with laboring in ways they have not been asked to, does not. I have a hearing loss myself, and it's extremely difficult for me to have conversations with people when I'm not wearing hearing aids, but nothing makes me more deaf than a preconceived notion about what's going on. I grieve the many times I missed out on what Jesus was speaking and what he made available to me because I decided in a given moment that I already knew what was right for myself.

In the gospels, Jesus often talked about his ultimate mission, the coming sacrifice; but he was usually met with the deaf ears of those who projected their own agendas on him, whether it was who he was, what he was meant to do, or what he came to offer them. Not Mary. Mary heard him loud and clear, and because she understood what Jesus was going to do, she understood what she needed to do; and she's once again found at his feet:

> *Six days before the Passover, Jesus therefore came to Bethany, where Lazarus was, whom Jesus had raised from the dead. So they gave a dinner for him there. Martha served* (figures) *, and Lazarus was one of those reclining with him at the table.*

> *Mary therefore took a pound of expensive ointment made from pure nard, and anointed the feet of Jesus and wiped his feet with her hair. The house was filled with the fragrance of the perfume.*
>
> *But Judas Iscariot, one of his disciples (he who was about to betray him), said, "Why was this ointment not sold for three hundred denarii and given to the poor?" He said this, not because he cared about the poor, but because he was a thief, and having charge of the moneybag he used to help himself to what was put into it. Jesus said, "Leave her alone, so that she may keep it for the day of my burial. For the poor you always have with you, but you do not always have me." —John 12-1-4*

In one extravagant act of worship, Mary anointed Jesus for His burial, breaking an alabaster jar of perfume at his feet and wiping his feet with her hair. It's claimed that the jar was worth a year's wages for a skilled laborer, estimated to be valued from 18,000–50,000 dollars. We always become like what we worship. What Mary did glorified Jesus because in that moment, Mary became like the subject of her worship—a God who loved us to the point of self-sacrifice, was receiving a form of worship that mirrored his sacrificial nature.

The love that Jesus gave Mary was returned back to him before the sacrifice even took place. This teaches us that we can actually praise God before a breakthrough takes place, because the breakthrough becomes visible to us through the magnification of his heart. We worship in gratitude, and we worship in faith.

Mary's demonstration of worship caused a reaction in the hearts of those around her, because extravagant worship always brings whatever is in our hearts to the surface. Judas accused him in a way that might make sense to many of us today:

*"Why was this ointment not sold for three hundred denarii and given to the poor?"*

Of course He only said this because he wanted the money for himself, but it demonstrates how many of us will reject forms of worship that do not make sense to us because we want to protect an identity of self-sufficiency, even in the place of worship. If we can control it, we can repeat it as often as we need to satisfy ourselves.

I remember one time I was at a retreat, and they had flags in the back during a worship night. I had a strong sense that I was supposed to grab one and wave it. At first I was hesitant, it just seemed like a girly thing to me, but eventually I went back there to grab one. I'm looking at these flags, and there are a few of different colors and designs; I chose a purple one because it's the color of royalty.

I stood on the side of the room and I began waving it, and soon after I began to see a shift that took place in the room; people began crying, some fell to their knees, and I felt the Holy Spirit come in power. Some people began crying out, and others began dancing. I never considered myself a flag person, and I haven't felt led to do this much since, but in that moment there was a specific form of worship that was placed on the heart to welcome the presence of God into the atmosphere and that worship actually moved his heart to the point of response. It was one of the coolest worship experiences I've ever had.

The point is, it was a specific form of worship for a specific moment. Worship doesn't always look like waving flags for me, in fact it usually doesn't. My worship is as fluid as my relationship with the Lord, it's not based on principle, but on intimate connection and obedience. Worship and wonder are meant to go hand in hand because it's always meant to be subject to the will of the Lord. We're always positioned under the mystery of his will, once the mystery is revealed, we respond in obedience. An obedient form of worship that is right for the moment in one season might be wrong in another. Worship should take place at the feet of Jesus.

In conclusion, this chapter is not meant to be a burden to you, but to paint a picture of what it looks like to free ourselves from our own expectations, and receive what the Lord has for us in a given moment. This liberty is an essential aspect of growing in trust with the Lord. When this type of trust is established, the things that seem natural to us no longer limit the way we engage with the Lord, or the world around us.

WHEN WE SIT AT THE FEET OF TRUTH, WE NO LONGER HAVE TO CARRY THE IMMENSE BURDEN OF DETERMINING OUR OWN DESTINY— MOST OF THE TIME WE DON'T EVEN KNOW WHAT WE WANT;

AND WE DEFINITELY DON'T KNOW WHAT WE NEED. I'M SO HAPPY THAT I GET TO DO MINISTRY FOR A LIVING, BUT WHEN I WAS A LITTLE KID I DIDN'T WANT TO DO MINISTRY, I WANTED TO BE A JEDI KNIGHT. THAT WOULD HAVE BEEN PRETTY COOL, I STILL WONDER WHY HE DIDN'T LET ME DO THAT.

# 7 OVER THE WATERS (PART 2)

I always find it fascinating that people respond in powerful ways to situations that seem devastating or totally hopeless. There's something that rises up on the inside of us in the most difficult scenarios. It's something attached to hope, but it isn't just hope, it's wonder. I've been in some slightly difficult situations during my lifetime, nothing compared to the things that many people have had to endure, but nonetheless challenging enough to push me past the boundaries of my previous limitations.

A few of these moments in my life went down in 2021. I had just graduated high-school, and decided I was going to join a Missions/Bible School program called *YWAM (Youth With A Mission). YWAM* has bases all over the world where they hold classes, and send missionaries into different atmospheres to minister the gospel. I knew a handful of people who have gone through the discipleship and sending program in the U.S., but this base that I went to was smack-dab in the middle of Kyiv, the capital of Ukraine. Leading up to this decision, I had never left the country before, or even lived on my own, but suddenly I found myself on a plane heading toward Eastern Europe.

After a brutal twelve hour flight from Chicago to Switzerland, and then Switzerland to Ukraine, I got out of the plane, went through security, and came out to a whole new world. I had heard people talk about culture shock before, but I had no idea what it could have felt like until that moment. The sun shone on my new environment as I went through the airport exit, and I realized I had just gotten into way beyond myself. I got picked up by a couple named Valeriy, and Nika, who put my luggage in the back of their van and then we began heading to their base. I'm not doing well; I'm trying to make small talk with them while I try to comprehend everything that I'm seeing around me. It's all different, the people, the architecture, the scent, the words on signs and billboards, nothing is the same, and I'm honestly feeling overwhelmed.

I put on a brave face, meet some of the staff at this school, for lunch I eat *borsch* (beet stew, not my favorite), and I'm taken to my room where I discover 6 bunk beds, and 11 other guys. That's fun. Slowly I figured out most of the students in my school don't speak my language, and it's going to be harder to make friends than I thought. That evening I go to bed, and silently cry into my pillow on the top bunk of my room. I'm praying, asking God how the heck he let me get in this situation, frantically thinking of any way I can get out of it, and eventually I just fall asleep.

When I woke up the next morning, I realized it wasn't a dream, I was really there. I took a deep breath, got dressed, and left my dorm room to find breakfast. I had no idea what this next season of my life was going to look like, but, I woke up that morning to a strange sense of peace about where I was at. I was completely in the hand of the Lord, all I could do was move forward.

Now that you've heard this story, I want you to imagine this: you're on a boat, in the middle of the sea, you're surrounded by 11 of the strangest dudes you've ever met; It's 4 AM, the boat is being tossed by waves and you're in the middle of a crazy storm. You're disoriented, dehydrated, the boat isn't getting anywhere. You're being hit with wave after wave, the wind is out of control, and you can't see anything. You start wondering if this is the day you're going to die; you hear shouts from the men around you: "Why did teacher send us out here!?" Mentally, you're spiraling. You begin to think maybe it wasn't such a good idea to follow this teacher guy after all; all of the sudden, you see him, the teacher walking past you—

on the water.

You're not feeling any more calm, you're actually freaking out. You think you might be hallucinating, then you realize the others see him too, they begin screaming: "IT'S A GHOST!" They're screaming, you're screaming; 55mph winds are crashing into your face and water is still splashing all over you; the teacher comes closer to the boat and you hear him speak:

*"Take heart; It is I. Do not be afraid."*

You're probably thinking: "Maybe I should be afraid, because that sounds exactly like something that a malicious, man-eating, sea-ghost would say." Not your buddy Peter though, he thinks it's cool that this guy is walking on the water; Peter says to Him:

*"Lord, if it is you, command me to come to you on the water." And the teacher replies: "Come."*

You watch as your friend, (who you already thought

was insane), literally gets out of the boat, and into the water that you're terrified of drowing in, and he doesn't sink, he's walking on the water too.

You pinch yourself, it's not a dream, you're actually there, and this is actually happening.

Now let's switch to Peter's perspective:

You're out on the boat with 11 other guys who think you're insane. You can't see, you're cold and wet, you're angry at your teacher for allowing this to happen; and now all of the men in the boat with you are screaming about a ghost; then you hear his voice– the same voice that called out to you at the beginning, when you were on the water fishing. And he says:

*"It is I, do not be afraid."*

A wave of peace fills your heart; you want to get closer to him. Part of you knows that if this man is who you think he is, all he would need to do is say the word, and you would be able to get on the water, and walk to him. You tell him to command you to come on the water; he says: *"Come."*

You're shaking as you put your leg over the boat, your foot touches the water, you feel it take your weight, and you're not sinking through. Slowly, you put your other foot on the water, and all of the sudden you're standing on the water staring at him, He's staring back at you. You take a step forward, waves are still crashing all around you, another step, and then another, you're getting closer to him. A big gust of wind hits you and almost knocks you over; you take your eyes off him, look around you, the danger of your environment grips your attention, and fear fills your heart. You begin to sink into the water, just before your head goes under water, you stretch out your arm and cry out: *"Lord save me!"* and your head sinks beneath the waves.

Suddenly you feel the warmth of his hand grabbing yours, He pulls you out; next thing you know, you're back in the boat, and the storm has ceased.

I just described the event that took place in Matthew 14. Oftentimes, we read this story and think: "Isn't it so amazing that Jesus walked on water?" But we often forget, Peter did too. That should spark wonder in your heart; the difference between Peter and the other disciples was that in that moment of total devastation and despair, Peter was able to tap into the hope that comes from God. He recognized the voice of the one who called out to him; it wasn't just the voice of a teacher, or a friend, but it was the voice of his heart's companion. The creator of the universe was calling out to him; the wildest wonders that Peter had ever witnessed were all attached to this one voice. He recognized the power of it, if this teacher only spoke the word, there was nothing stopping Peter from going out to him.

Our destiny is never limited by our natural limitations, it's only limited by our ability to recognize the voice of the one who calls out to us. In moments of trial, disorientation, or despair, things seem hopeless because we give our attention to the strength of the threat, and not the strength of our Lord, who fights for us. Peter was able to walk on water as long as he was mindful of the one who gave him the ability to do so. The moment when the threat became more real to Peter than Jesus, fear filled his heart and he began to sink.

The Prince of Peace rules and reigns wherever we're willing to give him a place to. If it's in our house, there he will reign, if it's in our schools, there he will reign. If we're willing to give him our bank accounts, our relationships, our workplaces, or even our minds, wherever we give authority to the Prince of Peace, he will establish peace.

When we're looking to establish peace in our lives, we often look in the wrong places. We'll try to figure out how to manage our way through the storm until the storm subsides, we stay in our boats or wherever we feel safest, and fight our way through. Peter saw the safest place as wherever Jesus was, even if it was out on the waters. The Bible teaches us that peace doesn't come from power, or control, it doesn't come from self-help literature, or algorithms to success; peace comes from proximity with this teacher, who establishes peace that surpasses our understanding.

The call to become like a child is a call to place our confidence in something beyond ourselves, to anchor ourselves in a force that exceeds our own abilities, a mind that surpasses our own knowledge. This is a call to a place of dependency, which positions us in places that are beyond our ability to stand on our own, places where we would drown if we weren't in the security of someone else's power.

The same God that hovered over the *chaotic waters* in Genesis 1, walked upon them in Matthew 14. Our God is a God that resides above the waters, he holds infinity in the palm of his hand. Everything that should, could, or will ever happen is considered by the mind of the Lord. The infinitude of anything deemed possible falls under his recognition and authority of God; there is no thing that we could dream of that exists outside of his ability to understand and accomplish. This revelation inspires us to actually trust him wholeheartedly:

*"Who is this, that he commands even winds, and water, and they obey Him" —Luke 8:25*

I'VE COME TO REALIZE THAT IN EVERY CHALLENGE, EVERY MOMENT OF DIFFICULTY, CONFUSION, ANXIETY, OR DEVASTATION, THERE'S AN INVITATION TO RECEIVE A GREATER REVELATION OF WHO GOD IS, WE JUST HAVE TO GET CLOSE TO HIM; THANKFULLY, WHEN WE DON'T HAVE THE STRENGTH TO DO SO, HE GETS CLOSE TO US.

On thanksgiving of 2021, in Kyiv Ukraine. I had been in the country for a while trying to do the missionary thing and make the most of the experience, but I hit a wall. Coming into the mission trip, I had heard rumors of revival, cool stories of things beginning to stir up around the city in Kyiv, I came excited to preach the gospel, expecting to see the multitudes get saved; but at this point I'm a few months in, and I've seen nothing. I wasn't doing well building friendships, I didn't feel like most of the people around me cared about seeing the Lord do amazing things; I felt useless and alone.

That night I got so frustrated I went on a walk in the middle of the night, I couldn't help but think about everything I had given up to be there: family, friends, soccer, all my favorite foods, hobbies, and my own room. I'm walking around at night in a really sketchy area, walking by stray dogs, dodging potholes filled with old cigarettes, praying to God, and questioning why I'm even there. Meanwhile my family is at home in Michigan, celebrating thanksgiving together, it turns out they don't celebrate thanksgiving in Ukraine. Eventually I sat down on a bench and just began weeping.

I had never experienced such a flood of doubt and insecurity in my whole life. I couldn't help but wonder if I even had a purpose, to me, nothing in my life made sense at that moment. All I could think about was how I was 5,000 miles away from anything I knew and loved. As I'm sitting on that bench wiping my tears off my face I felt a wave of peace wash over me, and I realized that it was his presence, he was there with me. He began to minister to my heart in a way I can't explain. I didn't come out of the encounter with any information about my future but he opened up a floodgate of revelation and insight to his own nature and the revelation I received in that moment had nothing to do with me and everything to do with him. That encounter left me with an abundance of hope, a genuine peace that I knew surpassed my own understanding.

This was a pivotal moment during my time in Ukraine, but even more so in the trajectory of the entirety of my life; I realized the Lord didn't bring me to Ukraine to labor for him, but to come to know him; the laboring would come later, and because of this season in Eastern Europe, the labor I get to do now comes from a much deeper place, and bears much more fruit. During that season of my life, the more I became familiar with the Lord's character, the more I came to understand what he was doing in a given moment, what he was saying. Eventually he began inviting me to say the things he was saying, do the things that he was doing. I began to understand the dynamic between Jesus, and the Father during his ministry on the Earth when he said:

> *"Truly, truly, I say to you, the Son can do nothing of his own accord, but only what he sees the Father doing. For whatever the Father does, that the Son does likewise. —John 15:19*

The Lord said: *"my sheep hear my voice"*. A sheep will follow a shepherd because they've become familiar with his voice; they've learned to trust it, and allow themselves to be guided from place to place, dwelling in the security of the shepherd's direction. We have to become intimately familiar with who our shepherd is, and establish trust with him if we are going to follow him wholeheartedly. My encouragement to you is this:

PURSUE THE KNOWLEDGE OF GOD AT ALL COSTS, BECOME HIS SHEEP, EMBRACE SEASONS WHERE HE POSITIONS YOU TO GROW IN TRUST WITH HIM; BECAUSE THAT TRUST IS ESSENTIAL FOR ACCOMPLISHING THE WONDERS HE WANTS TO DO THROUGH YOUR LIFE.

# 8 THE HELPER'S HEART

**D***ivine wonder is the threshold to divine encounter.*

If you don't know what a threshold is, it's that thin wooden slab that goes between two floors in a doorway as you leave one room and go into another; when you open a door, and step through its frame, you usually step past the threshold when you enter the next room.

Our wonder is often the threshold between our current understanding, and that which God has in store for us. You don't get the revelation without accessing the realm of wonder. So many people in our generation don't discover more about God, simply because they don't take the time to wonder about him.

This is why theology matters! *"Theology"* just means *the study of God; God is worth studying to those who care about pursuing a relationship with him.* This doesn't mean you have to know a ton of fancy words to describe the various doctrines and perspectives that have developed throughout church history, but you have to care about knowing God on a deeper level and pursuing that daily.

The problem I have with modern theology is that we often describe God in a way that seems apathetic about who he actually is. The way we describe God in circles of people who study theology deeply often would sort of be like if someone were to ask me to tell you about my wife, and I was like:

"Oh yeah my wife is Phoebe, she's 5'6" she has blonde hair, big blue eyes, and drives a silver Toyota Lexus."

You'd probably be like "Okay, but tell me about *her,* like what kind of a person is she? What is she like?" You might have an idea of Phoebe's outward appearance, but you'd have no idea what kind of a person she is. The same is true when we study God, if our theology doesn't unveil a deeper understanding of his heart, it's in vain; because knowing technical things about God doesn't actually edify us on its own if it isn't attached to his personal nature as a relational being. The knowledge of his heart produces security and satisfaction in our hearts. That trust with the Lord that can only be established by understanding his intentions reinforces our intimate relationship with him.

The enemy can make himself appear like God to us, so if our understanding of who God is doesn't go any deeper than his attributes it's much easier for us to be deceived. The highest priority of our lives has to be a daily pursuit of intimacy with him.

This chapter will be a combination of two things, a description of the divine nature of the trinity, and an invitation to explore the heart of God through the gift of Holy Spirit. I want us to study the Lord in a way that doesn't just give us head-knowledge to puff us up when we talk to people at church, but to study him in a way that opens up doorways to discovery of his heart. Let's brush up on our *pneumatology: the* study of Holy Spirit, Because the damage of drama around this topic and the secularization of Christianity has made it easier than ever to come to a misunderstanding of who Holy Spirit is. When we don't know who he is, we fail to recognize when he is at work; the key to partnering with Holy Spirit is knowing what he's all about. So, let's begin our journey of rediscovering ***The Helper's Heart.***

## The Person of Holy Spirit

Our God is one God, and three persons. This is where we get the word *"Trinity." Holy Spirit* is known as the third person of the Trinity, and he is exactly that, ***a person;*** He's not some stoic force like what Jedi use to push bad guys around in *Star Wars*, He's also not our magical Christian fairy dust that we use for our own purposes. He is ***God,*** and he is a ***person.***

As I've grown up in the church and experienced the body of Christ function in different ways, I've slowly come to realize that without realizing it, many churches have developed practices of abusing and objectifying the person of the Holy Spirit. Sometimes church leaders will either try to use Holy Spirit as some sort of personal pocket magician, while others neglect his existence entirely. The reality is that ***just because the Holy Spirit is in us, doesn't mean he agrees with us.*** As we grow in our understanding of who God is, it's necessary that we grow in submission to the Holy Spirit as well.

The best way that I have learned to understand who the Holy Spirit is, is by studying under the greatest *teacher* that has ever walked the Earth, ***Jesus himself.*** After all, He's the one who gave us the Holy Spirit as a gift in the first place, and He actually has a lot to say about it. In the book of John, chapters 14-16, we see Jesus begin to drop little bits of information on the coming of the Holy Spirit and his purposes for coming. At one point Jesus is sitting with the disciples and he tells them plainly:

> *"If you love me, you will keep my commandments. And I will ask the Father, and he will give you another Helper, to be with you forever, even the Spirit of truth, whom the world cannot receive, because it neither sees him nor knows him. You know him, for he dwells with you and will be in you." —John 14:15-17*

"In ME? GOD?"

Yes, in you.

The idea of God being on the inside of a person must have really thrown the disciples for a loop; I can understand why they didn't have much to say to Jesus in response. These disciples were young, and definitely were not the most theologically-educated in their community, but to anyone in their culture they would have been appalled by the idea of God living in them. They come from a culture where anyone who wanted to enter the presence of God would have to go through a huge list of rituals to purify themselves to even be near him without being obliterated, yet Jesus is sitting here telling them that the presence of God is going to dwell *in them*—that's wild.

An atonement that is so thorough, so complete, that God's presence would be able to dwell on the inside of someone was far beyond their own understanding. It's beyond mine, yet I live in it. They grew up in a culture where right-standing with God was something that has to be earned by themselves. I can't even imagine what kind of wonder these words of Jesus must have invoked in their imaginations.

Jesus goes on to tell them about the many purposes of the coming of Holy Spirit:

> *"The Helper, the Holy Spirit, whom the Father will send in my name, he will teach you all things and bring to your remembrance all that I have said to you. Peace I leave with you; my peace I give to you. Not as the world gives do I give to you. Let not your hearts be troubled, neither let them be afraid." —John 14:26-27*

Jesus says that Holy Spirit is coming to step into his role as our teacher, and that this teacher who is coming will bring to remembrance the things that Jesus has said to us from within us, and teach us how to walk them out in our daily lives. How cool is that? Through the Holy Spirit we literally have the words of Jesus abiding on the inside of us! In John 16, Jesus has another heavy, mind-boggling conversation with the disciples:

> *"I did not say these things to you from the beginning, because I was with you. But now I am going*

*to him who sent me, and none of you asks me, 'Where are you going?' But because I have said these things to you, sorrow has filled your heart."*
*—John 16:4-6*

I can't imagine the pain and confusion the disciples are dealing with when Jesus says these words. All twelve had all given up their lives because they met this man who gave them such joy, and purpose, incredible excitement, and indescribable peace. From the moment he first called out to these twelve men they began falling in love with him. They spent three years walking alongside him, becoming better versions of themselves, dreaming of everything they could do with Jesus and now he's telling them he's leaving. Pastor Bill Johnson once said while in tears:

*"A God that is everywhere wants to be somewhere– in Genesis, God would come in the cool of the evening, and walk with Adam; but not since the garden of Eden had anyone experienced what Adam did until these twelve men were chosen by Jesus, he was the living tree of life, he was with them day*

*after day after day; The atmosphere of heaven itself permeated their beings; they lost appetite for every other form of life."*

And now they're hearing him say he's leaving. What a heartbreak.

> *"Nevertheless, I tell you the truth:* ***it is to your advantage*** *that I go away, for if I do not go away, the Helper will not come to you. But if I go, I will send him to you." —John 16:7*

Imagine being at that level of intimacy with the Lord, and having him still say: "It's actually to your advantage that I go." What could possibly be better than walking with Jesus? What could this Helper be capable of that could somehow make the reality that the disciples were experiencing be inferior in comparison?

A couple years ago I had just started attending a school for ministry at my church, Radiant, in Kalamazoo, Michigan. I was at Culver's with some classmates in between classes, and one of those classmates I had just met, her name was Phoebe. Phoebe and I were getting along really well, and I thought she was beautiful so that had something to do with it. We're all sitting around a big table at *Culver's*, I'm listening to people talk, doing my best not to completely give it away that I was attracted to Phoebe (I gave it away), and then all of the sudden my attention is grabbed by this guy who's sitting at a table eating by himself. An intrusive thought pops in my head, in the form of a gentle voice that says

*"Hey, you see that man over there, his son just died."*

I ignored the voice, went back to the conversation, and I hear it again:

*"his son just died."*

Eventually I'm so focused on this guy that I'm not listening to anything around me anymore; eventually I just decide to get up and go talk to him:

"Hey this is going to sound weird, but I just wanted to ask, has anyone you're close with passed away recently?"

"Like, a family member?"

"Yeah", he didn't even look surprised that some stranger just came up and asked him this question, he just looked tired and sad,

*"My son just recently passed away."*

I was caught off guard, I had never had something like this happen before, and I wasn't exactly sure what to say. I just asked if I could pray for him; he agreed. As I'm praying for this man, I found that my prayers became more and more specific the more I prayed, it was as if the Holy Spirit was moving in my imagination, comforting and honoring this father for the role that he played in the life of his son. I began to speak words of assurance and hope; speaking against regret, shame, or any bitterness towards himself that might have come into his heart through the season of loss and suffering. As I mentioned before, disappointment makes us vulnerable; but God is near to the broken-hearted, I believe that he led me to this man.

I finished praying, and then I left. I spent a long time trying to figure out why that happened. I didn't really feel like I did anything all that helpful for the man who was grieving the loss of his son. As I was processing it I felt like I heard the Lord say: "In that moment I used you to comfort my son who was hurting, to show him that I see him, and I haven't abandoned him." I felt like he also said "This experience was for you as much as it was for him." And I realized that in that moment, I discovered what it looks like for the Holy Spirit to minister the heart of God through me in a unique way.

This was the first time I had ever gotten a word of knowledge for anyone, it was a beginning of a journey of walking in step with Holy Spirit. I learned that it wasn't at all a skillset, it was a gift; and Holy Spirit is willing to give gifts to those who seek them, and receive them humbly. Jesus was ministering on the

Earth today, through me. What a crazy reality. It's fun to encounter the love of God as he moves through you.

I love to see Holy Spirit move in supernatural ways that impacts the world around me, but I've learned he's much more focused on ministering ***to me*** than ministering ***through me.*** If there's one thing the Lord has taught me this last season of my life it's that he is much less concerned with ***what I'm doing,*** and much more concerned with ***who I'm becoming.*** Oftentimes, Holy Spirit is moving in our hearts, but we don't recognize it because we're too busy looking to see what he's doing in our environment.

Jesus continues to speak about the Holy Spirit:

> *"And when he comes, he will convict the world concerning sin and righteousness and judgment, concerning sin, because they do not believe in me; concerning righteousness, because I go to the Father, and you will see me no longer; concerning judgment, because the ruler of this world is judged." — John 16:8-11*

The work of Holy Spirit we all enjoy the least, but need the most is ***conviction.*** We love saying that God is our father until he actually fathers us, but the discipline of God is actually an inheritance we're given as his children, and it's an inheritance we're called to steward wisely.

Revelation 3 says:

> ***"Those whom I love, I reprove and discipline, so be zealous and repent." —Revelation 3:19***

If you're not being renewed in your understanding and corrected when you're wrong, ***you're not actually receiving the gift of the father's love.*** This is the process of sonship—to be brought up into the image of your father as you spend time with him and learn from him. The Holy Spirit grants us access to the fathers heart from within us.

Those who don't recognize their need for the sacrifice of Jesus don't really put their faith in him, ***so the Holy Spirit convicts us concerning sin.***

Jesus Christ was the perfect example of how to live rightly, so as he goes back to the father, ***the Holy Spirit convicts us concerning righteousness.***

And, because the ruler of this world is judged, ***the Holy Spirit convicts us concerning judgement.***

The conviction of the Holy Spirit is a gift we cannot neglect.

> *"I still have many things to say to you, but you cannot bear them now. When the Spirit of truth comes, he will guide you into all the truth, for he will not speak on his own authority, but whatever he hears he will speak, and he will declare to you the things that are to come. He will glorify me, for he will take what is mine and declare it to you. All that the Father has is mine; therefore I said that he will take what is mine and declare it to you. — John 16:12-15*

The Holy Spirit is the Spirit of Truth; and as we sit ***at the feet of truth,*** the Holy Spirit reveals that truth to us in our daily lives. As we walk in submission to the Holy Spirit, the truth of God is made manifest in our lives—changing the way we see others, speak to others, view challenges, and ultimately, it changes the way we view ourselves, not as orphans, but as children of the Most High.

The Holy Spirit is all about Jesus, wherever the Holy Spirit is made manifest, Jesus is glorified. The Holy Spirit plays a key role in the ministry of the gospel, because He ***wants*** to dwell in you and be with you:

> *In him you also, when you heard the word of truth, the gospel of your salvation, and believed in him, were sealed with the promised Holy Spirit, who is the guarantee of our inheritance until we acquire possession of it, to the praise of his glory. —Ephesians 1:13-14*

IF YOU'RE READING THIS AND YOU'VE NEVER ACCEPTED JESUS AS YOUR LORD AND RECEIVED THE GIFT OF THE HOLY SPIRIT, I HAVE GREAT NEWS FOR YOU—

*"If you confess with your mouth that Jesus is Lord and believe in your heart that God raised him from the dead, you will be saved. For with the heart one believes and is justified, and with the mouth one confesses and is saved."*
*—Romans 10:9-10*

I love the concept of wonder, but I don't believe Christians should have to wonder whether or not they're saved. Should you be willing to put your faith in the sacrifice of Jesus, a simple confession can confirm your eternal destiny; you can become sealed with the Holy Spirit and adopted by the Lord right now.

***Here's a prayer for you to follow:*** *(spoken out loud)*

***Jesus, you paid the price for my sins when you died on that cross, and you conquered my death when you were raised from that grave. Today, I choose to put my faith and trust in you. I turn away from my sin; I'll follow you and make you my Lord for the rest of my life.***

Welcome to the family—now, find a Bible-based church and share with someone there what you have done! Praise the Lord!

Now that we're all on the same page, let's talk about our *adoption.*

# 9 ADOPTION

In the early 1900s a new ideology was introduced to our society; A movement called *"Thelema"* (Thee-lay-ma), the greek word for *"desire."*

The fundamental principle they based themselves upon was: *"Do what thou wilt, is the whole of the law."*

This translates to: *"do whatever you desire."* and this ideology crept its way into our culture through communities of sorcerers, hedonists and satanists.

Now we live in a day known as *"the me era"* when those who were taught to serve themselves have learned to worship themselves. This wicked philosophy invaded our generation like a storm, disrupting communities, destroying marriages and families; while Satan, the leviathan, lurks hidden in the chaotic waters of a broken society where morality is subjective and the line between good and evil was blurred.

As a nation we became more and more obsessed with our own well-being, eventually taking our eyes off of God, fixing them on ourselves, and the Christian faith began steadily declining.

But over the last few years, Christianity has actually begun to make a comeback. We're beginning to see my generation, Gen Z, lead a massive restoration to church attendance; Bible sales are skyrocketing, and these people that were taught to put their trust in themselves are being confronted with their need for God.

I believe we are approaching the beginning stages of a nationwide revival, and I genuinely believe that our generation was created to lead it. But there is one thing that has to be addressed: our nation has been infected with an orphan mentality. Throughout the 1900s, when the percentage of people who walked with the Lord in our nation began slowly declining, a lie spread through our nation; it was the lie that they were fatherless.

Orphans often have a way of living that is reinforced by the idea that they have to fend for themselves. They'll learn how to get what they need from other people any way they can, they learn how to go without establishing emotional relationships with others. Many live in fear, worried that anyone who gets close to them is going to abandon them, or betray them; so they hold onto whatever they get a hold of tightly, and defend it aggressively. An orphan spirit has sparked movements in our society such as the sexual revolution where people began objectifying and ensalving themselves in the name of freedom and pleasure, or the roaring twenties when everyone began to work themselves to death fighting to be as wealthy as they possibly could.

To assume that the lies of the orphan spirit in our society haven't effected your world view at all would not be wise; but Jesus made us a promise:

> ***"I will not leave you as orphans; I will come to you. Yet a little while and the world will see me no more, but you will see me. Because I live, you also will live." —John 14:18-19***

At our core, everybody just wants to know they're recognized, accepted, and taken care of, after all, it's what we were created for. Most of us get to experience these things one way or another, but there are countless people, both old and young on the Earth right now that have no idea what it's like to have parents to feed them, clothe them, cry with them, or make them feel safe. They've never had anyone to teach them how to do things like have manners, ride a bike, or drive a car. There are multitudes of children that would do anything to have someone sit with them and read a story before bed, play catch with them, or have a family to wake up to on Christmas morning. But as far as they're concerned, they didn't qualify for that kind of treatment.

These children don't understand that they have an inherent value, or a purpose. They don't recognize that they should have been taken care of, that they deserve to be loved. They just assume they're not worth loving because that's what the world has taught them. For many of these kids, their parents abandoned them, or couldn't afford to look after them, so they've been in the foster care system for years (if they got lucky). They've gone from place to place, staying at one home until whoever they were with could no longer fill that role for them, then they go back to being orphans. They don't understand the social systems or financial circumstances happening around them, they just want to be loved.

Growing up, my little brother and I both had a best friend that was adopted. My friend's name was Max, he was adopted from Haiti, my brother's friend Shon, was adopted from Ghana.

Max and I haven't been close since 3rd grade, but I still think about him often. Max was always the happiest person in the room. He was in and out of surgery a lot because he had a medical condition in his leg that often had to be dealt with; he had a hard time running and spent a ton of time in a wheelchair, but still he was always the happiest kid in the room. I remember he would show up to my house either with crutches or a wheelchair and a huge smile on his face. We would play video games together, watch movies, and eat snacks. I loved being around him, I always felt like I could be myself.

Shon was always a ton of fun to have around. He and his cousin Kofi (also adopted from Ghana) would often come over and play soccer with me and my brother. We all loved soccer and played all the time, but Shon was really good, he would play so lightheartedly but amaze us as he did all these cool tricks and scored on us in crazy ways. Today he does it professionally but back then he was just doing it for fun. Both Shon and Kofi were always so grateful to be wherever they were, super kind, thoughtful, and easy to be around.

It seems like people who are adopted often get more enjoyment out of things, like living with a loving family, because they've experienced what it's like to go without one.

## Abba

The enemy looks for circumstances where he can use moments of rejection in our lives to convince us that we are not worthy of being loved. The orphan spirit watches for our most vulnerable moments of rejection or abandonment, and uses them to present the narrative that we're not loveable. The orphan spirit is a lying spirit that has had an affect on almost everyone in our society in one way or another.

Some of us have had abusive or manipulative parents, and that circumstance was used to present the lie that anyone we ever love is going to hurt us, lie to us, or use us for their own benefit. If someone has father wounds, they may not realize it, but when they hear other people call God *"Father"* they project the idea of the rejection that they have experienced in their lives onto the Lord. Because of that, many people ultimately reject God before they have to experience the pain of being rejected by him.

What those people don't realize is that the Lord actually does not reject them, he does not want to leave us as orphans, and we were created by a father that is absolutely flawless, from everlasting. He's unconditionally loving and infinitely willing to do anything for the well-being of his children, no strings attached. This is the kind of love that our hearts cry out for.

The enemy always works to dehumanize us. This is the only way he's able to rule the Earth. Every form of evil that the enemy has been able to sustain on the Earth is through dehumanizing one person in the eyes of another. This is how he convinces men to objectify and abuse women, how he convinces different nations to go to war with each other, or get people to steal from, manipulate, cheat, or enslave one another. Any kind of evil the enemy has ever accomplished through us humans he has done by first dehumanizing us in the eyes of each other.

WHEN THE ENEMY DEHUMANIZES US IN OUR OWN EYES, HE DOES SO TO GET US TO PICK UP THE YOKE OF SLAVERY. THIS YOKE OF SLAVERY IS THE IDENTITY THAT THE LORD HAS SPENT THOUSANDS OF YEARS CONFRONTING IN THE HEARTS OF THE ISRAELITES, WHO WERE ENSLAVED IN EGYPT, AND STILL DOES TODAY.

Apostle Paul went after this lie in Romans 8:

> *"For all who are led by the Spirit of God are sons of God. For you did not receive the spirit of slavery to fall back into fear, but you have received the Spirit of adoption as sons, by whom we cry, "Abba! Father!" —Romans 8:15*

When you received the gift of the blood of Jesus, you received the Spirit of adoption, by whom you cry out:

*"Abba" (Father).*

The Holy Spirit cries out from within you that you need the Father. I wish I could look every single one of you readers in the eye and say these words to you, ***"You are chosen." "You have been adopted."*** I'm trying not to cry in the middle of this cafe as I'm writing this.

You do not have to wonder anymore, what it feels like to be recognized, accepted, and taken care of; you do not have to wonder what it's like to be loved, you now have a helper to remind you this is true:

> *"The Spirit himself bears witness with our spirit that we are children of God." —Romans 8:16*

The Holy Spirit that dwells ***within you,*** testifies ***to you,*** that ***you are a child of God.***

The Holy Spirit is constantly crying out within you about the love that the Father has for you, such love that the Father would send his only son to die a brutal death for the sake of your ***adoption***. He doesn't just choose you, he chose you to the point where He's willing to make sacrifices to have you.

You are wanted, you are known, and you are loved. To God, you are worth the sacrifice. If you were the only one in the world to ever accept his Lordship, Jesus still would have gone to the cross for you.

## Groanings From Within

> *For I consider that the sufferings of this present time are* ***not worth comparing*** *with the glory that is to be revealed to us. For the creation waits with* ***eager longing*** *for the revealing of the* ***sons***

> ***of God.*** *For the creation was subjected to futility, not willingly, but because of him who subjected it, in hope that the creation itself will be set free from its bondage to corruption and obtain the* ***freedom of the glory of the children of God.*** *For we know that the whole creation has been* ***groaning*** *together in the pains of childbirth until now. And* ***not only the creation, but we ourselves,*** *who have the firstfruits of the Spirit,* ***groan inwardly*** *as we* ***wait eagerly for adoption as sons,*** *the redemption of our bodies.* ***For in this hope we were saved.*** *—Romans 8:18-24*

When I look back on my life, and I try to think about the defining moments that have made me who I am today, I think of a lot of different accomplishments and failures that I've experienced. But the moments that truly define my life have been moments where I did nothing, and God intervened.

One particular afternoon a couple summers ago, I was hanging out with a couple friends who were in the School of Ministry at *Radiant* before I decided to join, and they wanted to go to a prayer meeting at our prayer room in downtown Kalamazoo, so I joined them. I remember there were only a handful of other people in the room. One of them was the pastor who lead the prayer meeting, a few musicians, a couple other students of the school, there were one or two middle aged men, a mom who was playing with her kid in the back, and a few of our much needed intercessory grandmas. Thank God for them. This nation would have probably fallen apart already if it weren't for all the 70+ year old women praying for us every day.

At one point during the prayer meeting, I got on my knees and the atmosphere shifted. All of the sudden every feeling in my body went numb, every ounce of ambition dissipated, and I was left with nothing but a tender aching in the deepest places of my soul, ***a groaning.*** I had no words for what I was feeling, I just knew that I wanted to be with Jesus. I got up after that moment knowing only that whatever I had felt in that moment was the most real thing about me. I learned at that moment that at my core, the most significant thing about me is my desire to be loved by God, my need for it, and his desire to love me. Everything else that gives me meaning and purpose is predicated on those two things.

OUR LIVES MUST BE LIVED IN LIGHT OF OUR ADOPTION; WHEN THE ENEMY COMES WITH THE LIE THAT WE HAVE BEEN REJECTED OR ABANDONED, WE MUST CONTINUE TO TAKE THE WORD OF GOD WHICH REVEALS HIS NATURE AS A LOVING FATHER, AND APPLY IT TO OUR HEARTS DAILY.

Trust has three enemies: ***self-protection, self-promotion, and self-sufficiency.*** It's important that we identify the areas of our life where we don't trust the Lord, and reject the temptation to walk in these three things. When life doesn't go the way we expect, we have to trust the Lord's way is better. When we learn to rest in the safety of his will, we step into a process of the renewal of our minds, and our desires are slowly shaped to look more like his.

Maintaining a life of prayer is huge, not just for seeing God's will accomplished in our lives, but also for discovering what his will actually is! We don't always know what's best for us, and we don't always know what we should pray, but:

> *"the Spirit helps us in our weakness. For we do not know what to pray for as we ought, but the Spirit himself intercedes for us with groanings too deep for words. And he who searches hearts knows what is the mind of the Spirit, because the Spirit intercedes for the saints according to the will of God. And we know that for those who*

> *love God all things work together for good, for those who are called according to his purpose."*
> *—Romans 8:26-28*

*All things work together for good.*

I love Romans 8 because the passage lets us know that Jesus is praying for us, and then it tells us that the Holy Spirit is praying for us, and in between it says that *"all things work together for good."*

Wonder why.

Your father wants what's good for you; if you struggle to have faith for your own prayers, have some faith for God's prayers, because I'm pretty confident that God is not praying any prayers that aren't being answered accordingly.

## Grand Invitation

One day during the time of Jesus' ministry, the disciples were with him in Capernaum, and they asked him a question:

*"Who is the greatest in the kingdom of heaven?"*

I imagine Jesus grinning as he hears the question. So silly.

He looks over at a child who's sitting nearby, and summons the child to come stand in the midst of his disciples, I imagine the twelve men staring at the child with confusion, Jesus says to them:

> *"Truly, I say to you, unless you turn and become like children, you will never enter the kingdom of heaven. Whoever humbles himself like this child is the greatest in the kingdom of heaven."*
> *—Matthew 18:3-4*

In other words:

*"find a new way of thinking, a new perspective; at what point in your life did you decide that your worth was dictated by the way you measured up to those around you? Why are you competing with one another? Don't you know I have enough for all of you? Unless you humble yourself, ridding yourself*

*of this delusion of self-sufficiency and become like this child, you will by no means be able to receive the gift that I have for you; but whichever one of you is willing to humble yourself to the point of need, to become my dependent, you will be the greatest in my kingdom."*

My prayer for us is that we would all receive this invitation to become like children, to ditch the systems of comparison that steal our joy and reject the accusations that lie to us saying we don't qualify to receive what God has for us.

I believe that as many of you receive the invitation to become like children, you will begin to rediscover the greatest parts about who you are, unique characteristics that God placed on the inside of you before you were born. You'll uncover unique traits and passions from your youth, your mentality will shift first, then your behavior. Your parents and siblings will be able to recognize those characteristics from when you were a child and point them out, you'll discover your identity as God's chosen, and, for the first time in a long time, you'll feel safe enough to explore the realm of ***wonder.***

Many of you are going to change the landscape of your communities with creative expressions of *child-like wonder because the thief of comparison lost its grip on you.*

Those of you who accept this invitation are going to walk with such confidence and security throughout your lives that you will actually begin to get excited when obstacles appear, because you will look at those barriers and know there's an inheritance on the other side. And, for many of you, the gleam in your eye that disappeared many years ago will begin to shine again; your demeanor will shift, the people around you are going to feel safe or even excited when they look into your eyes because your attitude will demonstrate the love of God that you've personally experienced throughout your journey of growing in trust with him. My prayer for you is that the Lord would do a work so deep on the inside of you that when other people meet you, they encounter him.

I believe that the Lord is going to use the artistic expression of his children's worship to wage war against spiritual strongholds and principalities in regions all throughout the Earth. You are a partaker in the inheritance of an ***infinitely creative, infinitely wealthy, and infinitely loving God who has more in store for you than you could possibly imagine.*** Cling to the Lord tightly and hold everything else with open hands, it all begins with trust. Do not spend the rest of your life trying to replicate the things that you see around you; don't waste your life laboring for man's insufficient approval.

YOU HAVE BEEN GIVEN THE OPPORTUNITY TO BECOME TRANSFORMED INTO A UNIQUE EXPRESSION OF OUR CREATOR'S GLORY AS YOU BEHOLD HIM, IN AWE, AND WONDER.

DEATH TO FEAR, DEATH TO SELF-SUFFICIENCY, WE'VE BEEN ADOPTED.

For more information on

Jon's ministry, upcoming events

and to purchase his books,

go to:

JonNelsonMinistries.com